Modern Critical Views

Chinua Achebe
Henry Adams
Aeschylus
S. Y. Agnon
Edward Albee
Raphael Alberti
Louisa May Alcott
A. R. Ammons
Sherwood Anderson
Aristophanes
Matthew Arnold
Antonin Artaud
John Ashbery
Margaret Atwood
W. H. Auden
Jane Austen
Isaac Babel
Sir Francis Bacon
James Baldwin
Honoré de Balzac
John Barth
Donald Barthelme
Charles Baudelaire
Simone de Beauvoir
Samuel Beckett
Saul Bellow
Thomas Berger
John Berryman
The Bible
Elizabeth Bishop
William Blake
Giovanni Boccaccio
Heinrich Böll
Jorge Luis Borges
Elizabeth Bowen
Bertolt Brecht
The Brontës
Charles Brockden Brown
Sterling Brown
Robert Browning
Martin Buber
John Bunyan
Anthony Burgess
Kenneth Burke
Robert Burns
William Burroughs
George Gordon, Lord
  Byron
Pedro Calderón de la Barca
Italo Calvino
Albert Camus
Canadian Poetry: Modern
  and Contemporary
Canadian Poetry through
  E. J. Pratt
Thomas Carlyle
Alejo Carpentier
Lewis Carroll
Willa Cather
Louis-Ferdinand Céline
Miguel de Cervantes

Geoffrey Chaucer
John Cheever
Anton Chekhov
Kate Chopin
Chrétien de Troyes
Agatha Christie
Samuel Taylor Coleridge
Colette
William Congreve & the
  Restoration Dramatists
Joseph Conrad
Contemporary Poets
James Fenimore Cooper
Pierre Corneille
Julio Cortázar
Hart Crane
Stephen Crane
e. e. cummings
Dante
Robertson Davies
Daniel Defoe
Philip K. Dick
Charles Dickens
James Dickey
Emily Dickinson
Denis Diderot
Isak Dinesen
E. L. Doctorow
John Donne & the
  Seventeenth-Century
  Metaphysical Poets
John Dos Passos
Fyodor Dostoevsky
Frederick Douglass
Theodore Dreiser
John Dryden
W. E. B. Du Bois
Lawrence Durrell
George Eliot
T. S. Eliot
Elizabethan Dramatists
Ralph Ellison
Ralph Waldo Emerson
Euripides
William Faulkner
Henry Fielding
F. Scott Fitzgerald
Gustave Flaubert
E. M. Forster
John Fowles
Sigmund Freud
Robert Frost
Northrop Frye
Carlos Fuentes
William Gaddis
Federico García Lorca
Gabriel García Márquez
André Gide
W. S. Gilbert
Allen Ginsberg
J. W. von Goethe

Nikolai Gogol
William Golding
Oliver Goldsmith
Mary Gordon
Günther Grass
Robert Graves
Graham Greene
Thomas Hardy
Nathaniel Hawthorne
William Hazlitt
H. D.
Seamus Heaney
Lillian Hellman
Ernest Hemingway
Hermann Hesse
Geoffrey Hill
Friedrich Hölderlin
Homer
A. D. Hope
Gerard Manley Hopkins
Horace
A. E. Housman
William Dean Howells
Langston Hughes
Ted Hughes
Victor Hugo
Zora Neale Hurston
Aldous Huxley
Henrik Ibsen
Eugène Ionesco
Washington Irving
Henry James
Dr. Samuel Johnson and
  James Boswell
Ben Jonson
James Joyce
Carl Gustav Jung
Franz Kafka
Yasonari Kawabata
John Keats
Søren Kierkegaard
Rudyard Kipling
Melanie Klein
Heinrich von Kleist
Philip Larkin
D. H. Lawrence
John le Carré
Ursula K. Le Guin
Giacomo Leopardi
Doris Lessing
Sinclair Lewis
Jack London
Robert Lowell
Malcolm Lowry
Carson McCullers
Norman Mailer
Bernard Malamud
Stéphane Mallarmé
Sir Thomas Malory
André Malraux
Thomas Mann

Modern Critical Views

Katherine Mansfield
Christopher Marlowe
Andrew Marvell
Herman Melville
George Meredith
James Merrill
John Stuart Mill
Arthur Miller
Henry Miller
John Milton
Yukio Mishima
Molière
Michel de Montaigne
Eugenio Montale
Marianne Moore
Alberto Moravia
Toni Morrison
Alice Munro
Iris Murdoch
Robert Musil
Vladimir Nabokov
V. S. Naipaul
R. K. Narayan
Pablo Neruda
John Henry Newman
Friedrich Nietzsche
Frank Norris
Joyce Carol Oates
Sean O'Casey
Flannery O'Connor
Christopher Okigbo
Charles Olson
Eugene O'Neill
José Ortega y Gasset
Joe Orton
George Orwell
Ovid
Wilfred Owen
Amos Oz
Cynthia Ozick
Grace Paley
Blaise Pascal
Walter Pater
Octavio Paz
Walker Percy
Petrarch
Pindar
Harold Pinter
Luigi Pirandello
Sylvia Plath
Plato

Plautus
Edgar Allan Poe
Poets of Sensibility & the
 Sublime
Poets of the Nineties
Alexander Pope
Katherine Anne Porter
Ezra Pound
Anthony Powell
Pre-Raphaelite Poets
Marcel Proust
Manuel Puig
Alexander Pushkin
Thomas Pynchon
Francisco de Quevedo
François Rabelais
Jean Racine
Ishmael Reed
Adrienne Rich
Samuel Richardson
Mordecai Richler
Rainer Maria Rilke
Arthur Rimbaud
Edwin Arlington Robinson
Theodore Roethke
Philip Roth
Jean-Jacques Rousseau
John Ruskin
J. D. Salinger
Jean-Paul Sartre
Gershom Scholem
Sir Walter Scott
William Shakespeare
 Histories & Poems
 Comedies & Romances
 Tragedies
George Bernard Shaw
Mary Wollstonecraft
 Shelley
Percy Bysshe Shelley
Sam Shepard
Richard Brinsley Sheridan
Sir Philip Sidney
Isaac Bashevis Singer
Tobias Smollett
Alexander Solzhenitsyn
Sophocles
Wole Soyinka
Edmund Spenser
Gertrude Stein
John Steinbeck

Stendhal
Laurence Sterne
Wallace Stevens
Robert Louis Stevenson
Tom Stoppard
August Strindberg
Jonathan Swift
John Millington Synge
Alfred, Lord Tennyson
William Makepeace Thackeray
Dylan Thomas
Henry David Thoreau
James Thurber and S. J.
 Perelman
J. R. R. Tolkien
Leo Tolstoy
Jean Toomer
Lionel Trilling
Anthony Trollope
Ivan Turgenev
Mark Twain
Miguel de Unamuno
John Updike
Paul Valéry
Cesar Vallejo
Lope de Vega
Gore Vidal
Virgil
Voltaire
Kurt Vonnegut
Derek Walcott
Alice Walker
Robert Penn Warren
Evelyn Waugh
H. G. Wells
Eudora Welty
Nathanael West
Edith Wharton
Patrick White
Walt Whitman
Oscar Wilde
Tennessee Williams
William Carlos Williams
Thomas Wolfe
Virginia Woolf
William Wordsworth
Jay Wright
Richard Wright
William Butler Yeats
A. B. Yehoshua
Emile Zola

Modern Critical Views

JOYCE CAROL OATES

Edited and with an introduction by
Harold Bloom
Sterling Professor of the Humanities
Yale University

CHELSEA HOUSE PUBLISHERS
New York ◊ Philadelphia

© 1987 by Chelsea House Publishers,
a division of Main Line Book Co.

Introduction © 1987 by Harold Bloom

Printed and bound in the United States of America

10 9 8 7 6 5 4

∞ The paper used in this publication meets the minimum
requirements of the American National Standard for Permanence
of Paper for Printed Library Materials, Z39.48-1984.

Library of Congress Cataloging-in-Publication Data

Joyce Carol Oates.

  (Modern critical views)
  Bibliography: p.
  Includes index.
  Summary: A collection of critical essays on
this well-known American writer and her works.
  1. Oates, Joyce Carol, 1938–   —Criticism
and interpretation. [1. Oates, Joyce Carol,
1938–   —Criticism and interpretation.
2. American literature—History and criticism]
I. Bloom, Harold. II. Series.
PS3565.A8Z73 1987   813'.54   86-29968
ISBN 0-87754-712-2

Contents

Editor's Note

This book brings together a representative selection of the most useful criticism so far devoted to the work of Joyce Carol Oates. The critical essays are reprinted here in the chronological order of their original publication. I am grateful to Henry Finder for his erudition and judgment in helping me to edit this volume.

My introduction centers itself wholly upon *them*, my own favorite among Oates's novels. Walter Sullivan begins the historical sequence of criticism with an essentially negative view of the earlier novels, which he sees as being victimized by the phantasmagoric irreality in which we actually do live, and which Oates audaciously attempts to represent. In a review of *Do with Me What You Will*, Calvin Bedient salutes Oates as "a potent myth-maker in the drab guise of a social naturalist."

Wonderland, perhaps Oates's most ambitious novel, is read by Gordon O. Taylor as possessing a kind of autobiographical urgency, while G. F. Waller emphasizes instead the book's sense of the replacement of history by self-destructive passion. Eileen T. Bender, embracing Oates's rather generous view of literary influence as a health, rather than say an anxiety, sets forth the relations of three stories in *Marriages and Infidelities* to celebrated stories by Henry James, James Joyce, and Franz Kafka, relations that illustrate Oates's vision of the death of the ego.

Oates's moving sense of "terrified women," oppressed by physical violence and economic deprivation, is traced in an overview by Mary Allen. In a backward glance at Oates's first novel, *With Shuddering Fall*, Rose Marie Burwell uncovers the pattern of individuation (of a Jungian sort) that society always resists.

Bellefleur is reviewed by John Gardner as an ambitious allegory of joyful terror ebbing towards wonder, which he regards as the author's characteristic procedure as a novelist. In a parallel review of *Angel of Light*, Thomas R. Edwards sees Oates as returning from the fantasy of *Bellefleur* back to her more familiar territory, where the personal roots of public violence are exposed. Frederick R. Karl, reconsidering *them*, usefully compares Oates's Detroit apocalypse to the work of Dreiser. In a return to *Bellefleur*, Samuel Chase Coale judges that romance to be Oates's masterwork, and attempts to relate the book's achievement to Hawthorne and to Faulkner.

This book concludes with an eloquent tribute to Oates by Elaine Showalter, who analyses *Marya: A Life* as the novel that should begin the process of reconciling feminist critics and Oates, whose violent visions have not made her a favorite, until now, in feminist circles.

Introduction

There are no principles, whether of fiction or criticism, that oblige a novelist to be consistent in her or his vision, whether of art or of human life. Tolstoy is a massive instance of self-contradiction, but is not less powerful because of that. Still, it is remarkable that Joyce Carol Oates, fecund and imaginatively exuberant, should have espoused a moralist's stance that instructs us to accept limitations, in art and life, while simultaneously urging a vitalism upon us, a worship of the life-force. Oates has traces in her both of Theodore Dreiser and of D. H. Lawrence, novelists difficult to reconcile. Herself a lifelong campaigner against the American romance tradition, Oates frequently finds her own place in that tradition, presumably rather against her will, since she scarcely agrees with Emerson that the only sin is limitation. Concluding an essay on Lawrence's *Women in Love*, Oates seems both to summarize Lawrence and to intimate her own convictions, but I hear more Oates than Lawrence in this:

> How are we to escape history?—defy the death-process of our culture? With difficulty. In sorrow. So long as we live, even strengthened as we are by the "mystic conjunction," the "ultimate unison" between men and women, our lives are tempered by the ungovernable contingencies of the world that is no metaphor, but our only home.

That is eloquent, yet to call the world—social or physical—our home, even our only home, is itself necessarily a metaphor, though Oates will not acknowledge this. When Wallace Stevens, in *Notes Toward a Supreme Fiction*, tells us that the poem springs from our living in a place that is not our own, and much more, not ourselves, he is saying the opposite of what Oates says, and the place or world he cites is less a metaphor than is the world our home mentioned by Oates. It seems clear that Oates wants both

1

a denial of romance and an affirmation of the life-force of Lawrence, and she declines to see this double desire as being a deep split in her art.

Writing about Conrad, Oates has observed that he "sets up again and again in his novels dialectical struggles—melodramas of 'opposites'—that cannot be resolved except through the destruction of both, and the necessary deaths or defeats of his central characters." That is sometimes true of Conrad, and invariably true of Oates. Her novels indeed are "melodramas of 'opposites',," and their addiction to violence is therefore inevitable. Her subject is contingency, or the way things are, but teleology for her belongs to the domain of what Freud called the drives, love and death, so that her sense of factity, of our being imprisoned in over-determination, takes on the aura of a powerful mythology, as much her own as Freud's.

What I myself find most moving in Oates is her immense empathy with the insulted and injured, her deep identification with the American lower classes. She is not a political novelist, not a social revolutionary in any merely overt way, and yet she is our true proletarian novelist. Her outcast protagonists, such as Maureen and Jules in *them* (still my favorite among her novels), are the authentic children of the Great Depression, as I suppose Oates herself to have been. The epigraph to *them*, from Webster's *The White Devil*, sets what for Oates appears to be an open question: "because we are poor / Shall we be vicious?," and implies for her also its contrary: "because we are rich / Shall we be vicious?," a question perhaps answered in her novel *Expensive People*. I sometimes believe that the most interesting single page Oates has written is the "Author's Note" that begins *them*, and which certainly is part of the text of the novel:

> AUTHOR'S NOTE This is a work of history in fictional form—that is, in personal perspective, which is the only kind of history that exists. In the years 1962–1967 I taught English at the University of Detroit, which is a school run by Jesuits and attended by several thousand students, many of them commuting students. It was during this period that I met the "Maureen Wendall" of this narrative. She had been a student of mine in a night course, and a few years later she wrote to me and we became acquainted. Her various problems and complexities overwhelmed me, and I became aware of her life story, her life as the possibility for a story, perhaps drawn to her by certain similarities between her and me—as she remarks in one of her letters. My initial feeling about her life was, "This must be fiction, this can't all be real!" My more permanent feeling was, "This is the only kind of fiction

that is real." And so the novel *them*, which is truly about a specific "them" and not just a literary technique of pointing to us all, is based mainly upon Maureen's numerous recollections. Her remarks, where possible, have been incorporated into the narrative verbatim, and it is to her terrible obsession with her personal history that I owe the voluminous details of this novel. For Maureen, this "confession" had the effect of a kind of psychological therapy, of probably temporary benefit; for me, as a witness, so much material had the effect of temporarily blocking out my own reality, my personal life, and substituting for it the various nightmare adventures of the Wendalls. Their lives pressed upon mine eerily, so that I began to dream about them instead of about myself, dreaming and redreaming their lives. Because their world was so remote from me it entered me with tremendous power, and in a sense the novel wrote itself. Certain episodes, however, have been revised after careful research indicated that their context was confused. Nothing in the novel has been exaggerated in order to increase the possibility of drama—indeed, the various sordid and shocking events of slum life, detailed in other naturalistic works, have been understated here, mainly because of my fear that too much reality would become unbearable.

Since then we have all left Detroit—Maureen is now a housewife in Dearborn, Michigan; I am teaching in another university; and Jules Wendall, that strange young man, is probably still in California. One day he will probably be writing his own version of this novel, to which he will not give the rather disdainful and timorous title *them*.

One can guess that this is all no more or less fictive than the novel itself, which incorporates letters from Maureen to her teacher, Miss Oates. I recall my reaction to first reading the late James Wright's finest volume of poems, *Shall We Gather at the River?*, which has a searing vision of a city the poet evidently hated, "The Minneapolis Poem," and remember remarking to the poet that I wished he could be funded to go about our country in order to write *the* poem in dispraise of each of our principal cities. Oates's *them* is a grand negative rhapsody in dispraise of Detroit, possibly the most terrifying of all our urban hells. The "Author's Note" concludes with the prophetic intimation that Jules Wendall, who, rather than Maureen, clearly is Oates's surrogate, would give his version of *them* the less "disdainful and timorous title" of *us*, in a prolepsis of the novel's conclusion:

"And we don't have enough money now for ourselves. I . . . I'd give her some money if we had it, but . . . Jules, I don't want to remember any of it! A few bad dreams, that's all, nothing more . . . please. I wake up sweating and next to *this man*, a man I don't know, I mean I don't remember if it's my husband or not or some other man, someone who picked me up. I can't go through it any more, Jules, I'm finished. I'm going to forget everything and everybody. I'm going to have a baby. I'm a different person."

"Do you love your husband?"

"I'm going to have a baby, I'm a different person."

"What about Ma and the others?"

"What others?"

"Oh, you know, all of them—Ma and her brother, if he ever shows up, and Betty, and Connie, and Ma's crazy friends—"

"I guess I'm not going to see them any more."

Jules gave the back of her neck an affectionate squeeze. He seemed really quite joyful, a Jules she recalled from years ago, light on his feet and filled with surprises.

"But, honey, aren't you one of *them* yourself?"

She did not answer.

She had led him to the stairway, back to the stairway. Why didn't he leave! With one hand he reached out to touch the railing of the stairwell—it was plastic—and she saw how wobbly it was, ready to fall off if someone bumped against it. Thoughtfully, Jules drew his hand away. He said in a low, murmurous, almost ardent voice, "Sweetheart, I understand. I love you too. I'll always think of you, and maybe when I've done better, gotten on my feet, when I come back here and get married—I want to marry her anyway, that woman, the one who tried to kill me, I still love her and I'll make some money and come back and marry her, wait and see—when I come back, a little better off, we can see each other. All right? I love you for being such a sweet sister and suffering so much and getting out of it, using your head, but don't forget that this place here can burn down too. Men can come back in your life, Maureen, they can beat you up again and force your knees apart, why not? There's so much of it in the world, so much semen, so many men! Can't it happen? Won't it happen? Wouldn't you really want it to happen?"

"No!"

"Maureen, really? Tell me."

"No, never. Never."

He stood looking down at her. She pressed her hands against her ears. She was going to have a baby, she was heavy with pregnancy, but sure-footed, pretty, clean, married. She did not look at him.

"Well, I don't want to make life harder than it should be," Jules said.

He took his sister's hand and kissed it and said good-by, making an ironic, affectionate bow over her with his head: it was the Jules she had always loved, and now she loved him for going away, saying good-by, leaving her forever.

The genial yet grim question from brother to sister "But, honey, aren't you one of *them* yourself?" marks the final difference between Jules and Maureen. Whatever Oates's intentions, or his own, Jules will not become one of *them*, men and women trapped within contingency. He is a weird version of the portrait of the artist as a young man, but there we must locate him, another in the tradition that goes from Dickens's David Copperfield on through Joyce's Stephen Daedalus to many modern and contemporary incarnations. What again is his difference from his sister Maureen, which is to ask a fundamental question about Oates herself, who has affinities with both, yet more clearly resembles Jules.

"All of Detroit is melodrama," Oates has said in defense of *them*. In Oates's vision, most of America is melodrama or Gothic romance. That view would ally her to the formidable Flannery O'Connor, about whom Oates has written with great distinction, and who seems to me, more even than Dreiser and Lawrence, Oates's inescapable precursor. The conclusion of her essay on O'Connor's visionary art seems to me an eloquent manifesto of Oates's own radical, personally transmuted Catholicism, a Catholicism of apocalyptics and outcasts:

> O'Connor's revelations concern the mystic origin of religious experience, absolutely immune to any familiar labels of "good" and "evil." Her perverted saints are Kierkegaardian knights of the "absurd" for whom ordinary human behavior is impossible. Like young Tarwater, horrified at having said an obscenity, they are "too fierce to brook impurities of such a nature"; they are, like O'Connor herself, "intolerant of unspiritual evils. . . ." There is no patience in O'Connor for a systematic refined, rational acceptance of God; and of the gradual transformation of apoc-

alyptic religious experience into dogma, she is strangely silent. Her world is that surreal primitive landscape in which the Unconscious is a determining quantity that the Conscious cannot defeat, because it cannot recognize. In fact, there is nothing to be recognized—there is only an experience to be suffered.

It would not be fair to judge Oates by a close comparison with O'Connor's *Everything That Rises Must Converge* or *The Violent Bear It Away*. Except for Thomas Pynchon, no living American novelist and story-writer could sustain such a juxtaposition. Oates's *Son of the Morning* (1978) is her rough equivalent of *The Violent Bear It Away* (1960), and perhaps does not defend itself fully or evasively enough against O'Connor's masterpiece. When Oates says that small acts of violence in John Updike alarm her more than fiercer acts in O'Connor, she shrewdly accounts for the difference by noting that O'Connor is a parabolic writer. Since Oates also remarks that she interprets O'Connor's spiritual obsessions in a psychological mode, we are given a clue to Oates's violent visions, which are more intense even than O'Connor's. Neither naturalistic nor parabolic, Oates's narrative art partakes of both modes, while investing hope in neither.

Whether Oates will yet match the best of Flannery O'Connor seems to me very much an open question. I find *them* to be a permanent achievement, but remain uncertain about every other full-length novel she has published. Yet Oates is only forty-eight years old, and has daemonic drive and enormous writing energy. Her ambitions are large, and she has time enough to heal the twy-natured element in her work, which morally urges an acceptance of life's compromises while yielding always to the frontier drives of a life-force that rides over every compromise.

WALTER SULLIVAN

The Artificial Demon:
Joyce Carol Oates
and the Dimensions of the Real

In the fiction of Joyce Carol Oates, the middle ground is a no man's land into which her characters venture only occasionally. We know that in Detroit and New York and points south and west there are millions of people living ordinary lives on ordinary incomes, committing no murders, indulging no illicit appetites, requiring no psychiatric therapy or protective incarceration. But these are not the people who challenge Miss Oates's imagination. She wants hers either rich or poor, criminal or sick or drifting in that direction, with here and there a reasonably normal human being who might in rare instances earn the reader's unqualified admiration. To take one example, in *The Wheel of Love*, a collection of twenty short stories, a cursory count reveals ten cases of insanity or neurotic disability, three suicides, two attempted suicides, two murders, one death following criminal assault, and three violent ends which do not fit any of the above categories. To what extent this list might be augmented, should one keep score through all her books, I would not try to guess, for Miss Oates is surely the most prolific writer of serious fiction working in this country today. And in my judgment she is one of the most talented.

Two immediately apparent virtues of her work are those gifts which are indispensable to all writers of good fiction: an unerring eye and an infallible ear. Start with "Where Are You Going, Where Have You Been?" which is one of her most widely reprinted stories and justly so. In its basic delineations it is an interlude of terror: it builds fearfully toward a violence so unspeakable that it must happen offstage. Two boys in a jalopy come to call

From *The Hollins Critic* 9, no. 4 (December 1972). © 1972 by Hollins College.

on Connie who is alone at home on a summer afternoon. But one of the boys is a man, perhaps thirty, and this discrepancy in age—Connie is only fifteen—an old device used in a new way, increases the tension and deepens the meaning of the story. Youthful language and gestures employed by Arnold Friend combine with his uncanny knowledge of Connie's circumstances, the names of her acquaintances, the habits of her family, to develop a sinister adumbration. He is not what he seems, which is a familiar theme in modern fiction, and the car, the blaring radio, the clothes he has on, innocent symbols of a subculture under ordinary conditions, are made evil by Friend's illegitimate intention. This is the true terror as all good writers understand: we may be frightened by the distortions of a dream landscape; but horror resides in the transformation of what we know best, the intimate and comfortable details of our lives made suddenly threatening.

The story proceeds in conventional fashion. Miss Oates develops Connie in the opening pages and thus gives us our character over whom to grieve and with whom to suffer. We see her with her mother, with her schoolmates at the shopping center, with boys at the soda shop. The surface truth is drawn clearly and accurately and because of this some of the ambiguities of human existence—the kind of truth that the artist is trying finally to tell—begin to accrue to the story. Connie reaches out for adventure, deplores the humdrum, yearns for romance. That adventure should come in a deadly parody of romantic love is the sort of ironic trick that fate sometimes allows itself. Irony and violence are a part of life and they serve in this case to put youth in a new perspective. The young are at once more and less frivolous than we might formerly have believed, more and less innocent, but like all the rest of humanity, enormously vulnerable. Connie is helpless against the vicious Friend who enters her house and leads her away. There are to my knowledge no symbols here, but the story is rich with the imagery of life's deceptions and perils.

"Wild Saturday," which like "Where Are You Going, Where Have You Been?" appears in *The Wheel of Love*, is a story about a little boy lost in the selfishness and animosity of his parents. The mother is a cold citizen of the bourgeosie who despises her estranged intellectual husband and the feeling is mutual. Saturdays are the days that Buchanan spends with his father, and this Saturday begins as we know all the others do, with a sense of release that follows his mother's furious last kiss and the hope that this time things will be different. The usual trip to the zoo is promised, the picnic lunch, but first they must get Sonya, Dad's girlfriend, and her fatherless child, Peter. Then there is Artie, a potter, who hates children and just about everything and everybody else in the world to judge from his conversation, so as usual they do not go to the zoo, but to Sonya's apartment, where the fat girl who shares the apartment with Sonya greets them.

There is nothing to entertain Buchanan here. Sonya and Dad argue; the picnic basket yields only candy and potato chips; Sonya's flatmate claims to have flu. Visitors come and go. Wine is poured. At last Buchanan retreats to the tiny bedroom where Peter is already sleeping and sleeps himself and awakens with a cold. Peter has wet the bed; Sonya is half undressed and drunk; Dad is unconscious on the living room floor and cannot be aroused by the police who come looking for Buchanan. But to the very end Buchanan is loyal and will not admit to his outraged mother that he has not been to the zoo.

This story lives in the sharpness of its characterization. Buchanan is a perceptive, honest child, not above a thrust of impudence now and then. He is largely innocent and therefore victim: he becomes for his mother and father a weapon for each to use against the other. And what is worse, each tries to justify his own life style by imposing it on Buchanan. The story is one of selfishness compounded by dishonesty and the attitudes are so splendidly cast, the dialogue is so accurately devised that the narrative is profoundly convincing. Sonya's sympathy is engaged by strangers seen on the street, she proclaims her love for her baby when she is drunk, but she will not prepare a dish or change a bed or find a lost shoe for Peter. So it is with the others, with Dad who will not give Buchanan a moment of his undivided attention and with Buchanan's mother who wants most of all to deprive Dad of Buchanan's company forever. Except for Buchanan, who is hardly old enough to be evil, there are no good people here, and certainly there are no winners. Life that was tense and drab at the beginning of the story is worse at the end. Even the mother, who has won Buchanan from his father, has lost a little more of the slight affection her son once had for her. And of course we see ourselves here, whichever side we are on, whichever path we choose for our lives to follow.

From *The Wheel of Love*, I take a final example. "Bodies" shows Miss Oates in her bizarre dimension. Pauline, rich, young, a sculptor and instructor at an art institute, is pursued by a man of uncertain background. She does not know quite what he wants from her, other than her company which she is unwilling to give, and in a scene that is uncommon, even for Miss Oates, he accosts her. On the street, in the light of day, he cuts his own throat, sinks to his knees, clutches Pauline around the waist and lets his blood spill out upon her. The end of the story is this: Pauline, who cannot forget the blood on her stomach and thighs, believes she is pregnant and cannot be dissuaded. She is sent to an institution and is given little chance to recover.

I do not want to pursue all the ramifications of this story. The meaning of its main action is obvious at least to a point: a marriage of death and birth which issues into insanity—but an insanity modified, the irrational quality softened by its relationship to art. For the story is couched in terms of artistic representations of life, death, fate, love: and of dreams which are composed of remembered objects of art, sculpture, painting; and of visions of violence. Art, too, is perhaps a manifestation of insanity and the artist an abnormal figure in the world's eyes. Finally, we suspect that life itself, when it is seen in all its breadth and intensity is partly insane, even as it maintains our rational context. However this may be, however far we may want to proceed along this course of inquiry, of one thing we can be sure: a narrative such as "Bodies" is the place to begin. Of the three stories I have examined here, it is by far the most typical of Joyce Carol Oates's fiction.

II

It would be too much to say that the spirit of *tour de force* informs the art of the short story. Yet, we are all familiar with the difficulty the best short story writers occasionally encounter when they try to write novels. Many of the characteristics which are virtues in short fiction—the clarity of dialogue and detail, some kinds of wit—become mannerisms that sometimes test the patience of the reader when they are employed on a large scale. And technical devices that will work for ten or twenty pages, will not necessarily survive for four or five hundred. I have in mind the kinds of thing Miss Oates attempts in *Expensive People*, an early book, and in *Wonderland*, her most recent novel. *Expensive People* is a tale told by a slob, a fat and neurotic post-adolescent who cannot and is not intended to convince us that his story is true. Richard Everett begins his first person narrative with a bad pun: he calls himself a child murderer and then must explain that he means a child who kills, not one who murders children. But is he really what he claims? We never know. It is true that a sniper is loose in Cedar Grove and the fact that Richard's mother is shot to death is established. But the police do not find the rifle where Richard tells them he has hidden it, and at the end of the novel, the psychiatrist says, "Richard, let me assure you of this: hallucinations are as vivid as reality, and I respect everything you say. I know that you are suffering just as much as if you had killed your mother." So, having paid the price by reading the book in the first place, the reader can make his choice.

Miss Oates may be suggesting that objective reality does not matter, that appearance is all. But the case does not seem quite that simple. Richard calls his mother Nada—such a name can hardly be without philosophical implications—and she is a fine example of how surface impressions deceive. She presents herself as Natashya, the daughter of Russian nobility, now dead. But as we discover, she is really Nancy Romanow and her immigrant parents survive her. Perhaps then, there is no way to know reality, or perhaps reality is what we make it, what we say it is. Or maybe the book is not about the real at all, but about guilt and intention and the moral structure of the human act. Whatever the theme was meant to be, it is one that might have served very well for a short story, but it is not substantial enough to sustain a book.

Wonderland, a more difficult and more skillfully conceived book, may be even more of a failure as a novel. The volume is dedicated to "all of us who pursue the phantasmagoria of personality," and having devoted a good deal of time to Miss Oates's narrative, I am as yet uncertain as to whether I want to count myself in or out of that distinguished group. Which is to say, I do not know quite what she means. If personality is a phantasmagoria, then what is character, or more to the immediate point, characterization? If we take this as a strictly literary question, the answer will be, It depends. Short stories do not make the same demands for development and motivation that novels make. For example, Miss Oates has written a story titled "You," which exhibits her talents at their best. The main character is a television actress, aging but still beautiful, famous, but not at the center of the world's renown. She is miserable because of her selfishness and all those around her are miserable for the same reason, and nothing changes her, not even the attempted suicide of one of her daughters.

The narrative is given texture by a dual point of view. Marion tells her mother's story in the second person while she tells her own in the first and the two fictional movements form a counterpoint of carelessness and responsibility. The two women, as well as the minor characters—the other daughter, Miranda; Peter, once the mother's lover, now Miranda's—are very clearly drawn and totally believable, as Miss Oates's people almost always are *at any given moment in their careers*. Where the mischief comes is when Miss Oates attempts to take a character such as Madeline Randall of "You" beyond the limits of a situation which is strictly circumscribed. In the novels the characters simply change. Personality does become a true phantasmagoria, not an organic development from stage to stage, but a random shifting from one manifestation of character and being to the next. As I shall try to show later, her best novels, *A Garden of Earthly Delights* and *them*, are marred by this discontinuity of attitudes and values, but what had before seemed a defect in craftsmanship emerges as a philosophical principle in *Wonderland*. By a series of clever devices, disruptions based largely on chance, the main character is carried from one to another of a set of vastly disparate circumstances. With each dislocation he becomes a different person to the extent that even his name is changed. The idea is not good; it does not work; even the writing, the details of setting and action which are usually Miss Oates's strong suit, fails to convince.

III

A Garden of Earthly Delights and *them* share a common glory—Miss Oates's talent for clean fictional representation—and a common difficulty. One does not know where the focus should fall in these novels or who the main characters are. *A Garden of Earthly Delights* begins among itinerant farm workers whom we follow from Arkansas to Florida to New Jersey and back to Florida once more, and the first third of the book clearly belongs to Carleton Walpole. In the opening pages, Carleton talks of making enough money to pay off his debts and return to his small farm in Kentucky, but this ambition is soon forgotten, and the novel succeeds in showing the very directionlessness of Walpole's life. He works, breeds, drinks, fights, and his days drag on leaving him nothing to show for the effort he has put into living and no hope for a future that will bring him any sort of ease.

There is no way to exaggerate the brilliance with which the sordid quality of Carleton's existence is conveyed. The hovels in which the workers live, the food they eat, the clothes they wear—all the mundane details are drawn vividly and with economy. The dialogue rings true, the people are convincing. We see Carleton's wife grow more and more withdrawn with the birth of each of her children until she bleeds to death after her last delivery. Such a thing should not have been allowed to happen, the doctor admonishes later, but we are by this time almost inured to the unceasing agony these people undergo. Pearl is buried, Carleton finds another woman, life continues in its old pattern; the children grow up foul-mouthed and dirty and take their places in the field.

At the end of the first section of *A Garden of Earthly Delights*, Carleton dies, but by this time the emphasis of the narrative has shifted to his oldest daughter. With the help of a kind man who for a long time will not accept the physical love she offers him, Clara escapes to a small town, lives in a rented room, works at the five and ten. Once more, Miss Oates's vast talent for conveying the hard circumstances of insignificant and impoverished lives engages us absolutely. Clara strives for beauty. She skimps to buy a bed-spread, sews curtains on Sunday afternoon, cherishes a cheap pair of shoes, a tawdry ribbon. It is only after she is translated from poverty to ease and security, first as the mistress, later as the wife of a rich man that the novel begins to falter.

For though life may be without purpose, as Miss Oates's fiction generally seems to assert, it nonetheless usually assumes a certain shape. Days lived under any kind of ordinary circumstances form a pattern and this pattern helps establish the texture of a novel. Motivations develop, relationships mature and shift, aims are pursued, actions are taken, consequences are suffered. But these are ends that Miss Oates will not seek in her work. In *A Garden of Earthly Delights,* accidents happen, blood flows. One of Clara's stepsons dies in a hunting accident. Her own son kills his father, then shoots himself. There are sexual encounters, arguments, fights, accommodations, but except for the fact that we continue to read about the same group of characters, the incidents and sequences appear to be separate unto themselves. And soon, the seemingly inevitable disintegration toward mental illness sets in.

Now, I am aware of the argument, all too frequently heard these days, that in order to portray a chaotic world, we must resort to a chaotic art. There are enough writers around who have followed this notion to its conclusion to show us how fallacious it is. Art as an imitation of life does not mean art as a carbon copy of life, and one of the first tasks of the writer is to maintain some kind of control over his material. He does this by giving the material coherent shape. But of equally serious consequences to her fiction is Miss Oates's tendency to let her people go insane. Here again, I think I get the point. She is saying that we are all crazy to one degree or another, and in taking this position, she puts herself in agreement with much modern psychological and even judicial theory. There are no longer the good and the evil among us, but merely the sick and the well. This is not the place to examine such a view of human morality, but I do submit that should it gain complete hegemony it will be the death of art.

Literature requires action that is morally significant, which means that the characters must be at least theoretically free to choose for themselves. If we are persuaded that Macbeth murdered the king simply as a result of some psychosis which forced him beyond his control into regicide, then the play makes scant sense. What was true for Shakespeare is, I think, true for Joyce Carol Oates. Once a suggestion of lunacy is allowed to intrude, then doubt is cast over all the procedures of a novel. Where did the neurosis begin? What actions and choices were tainted by it? To what degree has the fiction become nothing more than a case history? Finding Clara in an institution at the end of *A Garden of Earthly Delights* gives me no sense of fulfilment. It is a sad fading away of a book that contains much that is powerful and sharp.

IV

Them is more ambitious than *A Garden of Earthly Delights*—it has more characters, its scope is wider—and as a chronicle of life among the poor of a big city, it rings all too true. We are told in an author's note that the material for the book, including not only the characters and plot, but much of the voluminous mass of details which give the novel its intense verisimilitude, were told to Miss Oates by one of her students at the University of Detroit. Where it was possible, Miss Oates says, the recollections of the student were "incorporated into the narrative verbatim," but this is not necessarily an easy way to write a novel. The trick is to know what can be used as is, what must be discarded, and what the author must furnish for himself. In other words, the problem of form remains, the parts must add up somehow to make a whole.

In *them*, there are a good many parts to be accounted for. The book begins with typical Oates blood and thunder. Loretta, young and poor and dissatisfied with her lot, takes her first lover and wakes the next morning to find the boy dead beside her. He has been shot by her brother. The policeman whom Loretta calls off the street first makes love to Loretta, then helps her dump the body in an alley. Later Loretta and the policeman are married and their relationship is a proper overture for the sordid scenes that are to come. In the progress of the book, Loretta is displaced as principal character by her son Jules, who in his turn gives way to Loretta's daughter Maureen. But until the last phases of the narrative are reached, Miss Oates keeps fairly good control over most of the various ramifications of her plot.

And the writing in *them* is certainly some of the best she has ever done. Maureen is a superbly drawn character. We know her first as a sad, quiet girl trapped in poverty, surrounded by loud, insensitive and vicious people. Her brother can escape by taking to the streets, but for Maureen there is only the temporary respite found in books, and her reading is continually penetrated by the complaints of her grandmother, the scolding of her mother, the verbal and physical assertions of her aggressive sister. We watch the brutalization of this perceptive and innocent and essentially decent child. When she is denied use of the library until a twenty-five cent fine is paid, she is terrified that her only solace might be taken from her forever. Having been elected secretary of her class in school, she loses the minute book and searches in vain and in agony for it. These sequences succeed absolutely. They transcend themselves and become images of our general loneliness and spiritual isolation. Miss Oates avoids sentimentality by the simple expedient of telling the cold truth.

Maureen's fate is her will to escape the shabbiness of her life. Her career as a prostitute ends when her stepfather discovers her cache of money and beats her severely. She falls into mental illness—that most familiar of all ailments in the Oates canon—recovers, gets a job as a secretary, moves to the same sort of cheerless room that Clara occupies in *A Garden of Earthly Delights*. She enrolls in a night class at the university extension, discovers in her teacher the man she wants to marry and induces him to leave his children and his wife. She gets what she thinks she wants. When we last see Maureen, she is pregnant and worried over money, since so much of what her husband makes must go for alimony and child support. In my judgment, the conclusion of Maureen's story is not written with the depth and complexity that endow so richly the earlier scenes in the book. This may not be totally Miss Oates's fault. Love is at best difficult to write about: there is a sameness to it; lovers everywhere are inclined to think and talk alike. The urge arises. Somehow, somewhere fancy is bred. But how distinguish one urge, one love from all the rest?

The distinction is partially made by the circumstances that surround the development of affection. And by the motivation, which in Maureen's case is firm and sure and one of the best aspects of this part of the narrative. Her desire is not so much an overwhelming passion for the plain professor, but for what he represents in the scheme of her future hopes: she wants a home of her own, a husband, a child. She does not find herself incurably in love with a married man: rather, she chooses him with *sang froid*, feeling no more concern over the fact of his marriage than she feels over the drape of his necktie or the color of his shirt. She captures him simply by going after him, and I suppose we are convinced, if a little surprised at his vulnerability. She, the indifferent student, calls on him in his office and allows him to allow the conversation to repeat itself while beneath the empty, almost silly words, their relationship makes its steady course. This is good work. Only in terms of my earlier comparison does it appear to be inadequate. It seems contrived in relation to the sounder parts of the story.

I think Jules is less successfully drawn than Maureen, which is perhaps a result of the ordinary perils of characterization. Like a good many female writers, Miss Oates may not portray men as well as she portrays women, though I find Carleton in *A Garden of Earthly Delights* convincing enough.

Jules too is believable as a young man, enduring some of the same agonies that Maureen endures, but endowed, because he is a boy, with better opportunities to escape their common fate. He drops out of school, finds a life on the streets, flirts with girls, gets money. But then Miss Oates begins to indulge her taste for the bizarre and Jules becomes not so much unreal as insignificant, unrealized in the ultimate fictional sense. He falls into a relationship with a nervous, mysterious stranger, whose source of livelihood is unknown and whose comings and goings are seemingly without purpose. While Jules works for Bernard Geffen, he meets Nadine.

Or rather, he sees her for the first time when he drives Bernard, who is her uncle, to her parents' home in Grosse Point. At his first glimpse of her, Jules is enchanted with Nadine's beauty—the magic attractiveness of this school girl in knee socks. But he does not meet her until after the strange Bernard has been murdered by gangsters and Jules has a job delivering flowers. Catching sight of her one day on a Detroit street, he hails her, offers her a potted plant, tells her that he loves her. The affair thus begun receives a long development. Jules and Nadine run away together. He supports her by stealing, but he gets sick and she abandons him. Later, when they meet again, she is married and Jules is working for his affluent uncle. Here the decline toward neurosis and violence begins.

Perhaps I have read too much of Miss Oates's work in too short a period of time, but I do get a terrible sense of futility, not to mention *deja vu*, watching pair after pair of her characters degenerate into insanity and the shedding of blood. They love and love again, these particular lovers: then on the bright morning after their night of passion, Nadine shoots Jules as they walk together down the street. "The spirit of the Lord departed from Jules," Miss Oates tells us, and I assumed on first reading that Jules was dead. Such is not the case. He survives, and later regains this lost "spirit of the Lord." The end of the book plays itself out: life goes on and Jules drifts through it. He becomes one of the street people around the university, takes in a runaway girl, abuses her and forces her into prostitution. After a race riot, in which Jules kills a policeman, we have one last account of him as an organizer for a leftist group. And the novel is over.

My frustration in trying to deal with *them*, the divisions that cloud my judgment of it are indicative of my view of Miss Oates's fiction taken as a whole. I have already declared how well I think Miss Oates writes. Her best stories are among the very best written today, and *them* is replete with fully realized scenes and compelling emotional intensity. About life's small defeats and lesser triumphs, Miss Oates almost never fails to tell the truth. It may be that perfection on a small scale is the proper fruit of Miss Oates's talent. The accomplished writer of short fiction who fails when he attempts to work in the larger dimensions of the novel is, as I have said, a familiar figure of our time. But I think there is also a problem of vision involved here, part of it the temper of the age, part of it Miss Oates's own view of the world and time in which she lives.

In *The Edge of Impossibility*, a collection of perceptive and persuasively written essays on modern literature, Miss Oates is concerned with the possibilities for writing modern tragedy. She thinks that tragedy can be written, though it is necessarily circumscribed by our place in history—what I, but probably not Miss Oates, would regard as the deficiencies of our age. She puts her case this way:

> If communal belief in God has diminished so that, as writers, we can no longer presume upon it, then a redefinition of God in terms of the furthest reaches of man's hallucinations can provide us with a new basis for tragedy. The abyss will always open for us, though it begins as a pencil mark, the parody of a crack; the shapes of human beasts—centaurs and satyrs and their remarkable companions—will always be returning with nostalgia to our great cities.

Or to put this another way, the modern hero, placed irrevocably beyond good and evil, must create himself. This necessity for self-creation is at once his doom and his only avenue to freedom; he must transcend his society and in the process he will destroy himself.

This is not the occasion to attempt to trace the ramifications of such a theory, nor do I want to end by saying that Miss Oates's work is a mere demonstration of the perils and the advantages of existentialism. This would be to oversimplify, for writers are not merely the product of what they think: if they were, many of our best ones—Tolstoy, for example—would have been diminished. But what Miss Oates says about Mann and Ionesco and literature in general does suggest that our frantic circumstances inform our frantic art. There can be no question that life as we live it, as Miss Oates describes it, is enough to drive us crazy, but does this mean that we must continue to write the same story over and over—a chronicle where violence is a prelude to total spiritual disintegration and the only freedom is the total loss of self? Perhaps so, if Miss Oates is accurate in her perception of our modern condition. But I can offer no final answer. I wish I knew.

CALVIN BEDIENT

Sleeping Beauty
and the Love Like Hatred

Joyce Carol Oates's novels are grinding, brutal, harsh. She is the mistress of panic, knowing its taste, its "first sharp darts," the new pulses it surprises on the body, with an alarming thoroughness. No one, not even Lawrence, has so given the novel over to extreme states of feeling. She writes from within psyches that are like prehistoric organisms, creatures all spines and terrible soft undersides, engaging in love that is like hatred, combat that is like love, mercifully separating, re-engaging. . . .

Oates is a potent myth-maker in the drab guise of a social naturalist. She releases the stuff of nightmares in the raw streets of Detroit. The focus of her myth—like that of Emily Brontë and Lawrence—is the greed, the overreaching, the "experimental" excitement, in human relationships. She rows in the rapids of hunger. It is often just as hard to believe in the passions she depicts—and just as hard not to—as in those of Brontë and Lawrence. But where the latter give us poetic universes shot through with desire, Oates makes psychology swallow everything. Descriptions of *sensations*, her novels are fiercely claustrophobic, and you experience them like a privileged sickness.

Oates imagines so deeply from within the aboriginal core that physical scenes are like irritating films on the eyeball, social questions largely words *out there,* surprising when they seem to be one's own. Though civil rights and Zen-colored philosophy are issues in *Do with Me What You Will,* though much is said about the law, nothing is enough like belief to test the

From *The New York Times Book Review,* (14 October 1973). © 1973 by the New York Times Co.

reader, and the wheels of dialectic fail to mesh. Like the doctors in *Wonderland*, Oates's preceding novel, the lawyers here are so motivated by what *they* need—power, a swollen identity—that their public statements smell of camouflage for the hidden creature.

Oates's obsessive biological cynicism is so feral and has kept her prisoner so long in its lair that she has begun to plot a way out. In recent bold essays she derides the suicidal end of the "Renaissance ideal" of a separate "I," the paranoid protagonist in a drama staged between itself and everything else. Like Lawrence she wants a "field of living spirit" back again. "Miss Plath's era is concluded," she says flatly. But Oates's previous novels are, after all, huge cousins to Plath's brilliantly savage poems (indeed, Plath's novel, *The Bell Jar*, is uninspired Oates). And the interesting question in reading her new book has been whether she could coax her dark imagination out into the light of day.

In a startling way she succeeds—not by opposing her instinctual cynicism but by accepting it. At the end of *Do with Me What You Will* she brings its face out into the light, dazzled, blinded, saving it by love—as Ariadne might have saved the Minotaur, where Theseus, in his fear, had to slay it. The essays, with their high repudiation of "Romanticism," show the hand of a Theseus. But the daemon of this novelist is vitalist or it is nothing, and where a god may have been called, a devil has rushed in.

Far from attacking "selfish" veins, Oates takes their part, Promethean, against a still more terrible cynicism: the defeatism under which the earlier novels groaned. Prompting the self out of its "childhood fears of annihilation and persecution," she girds it and sends it out greedily—in Romantic fashion, though without fragrant illusions—to encounter, indeed to raid, reality. She rubs the Renaissance ideal back to combative health.

The novel traces, if with narrative broadenings, the dumb, dreamy, intermittently panicked progress of Elena Ross into existential risk, sexual aggression. She is one of those women so inertly and incredibly beautiful that men want to burrow into them as if into immortality or perfection. Indeed, until provoked to stricken sexual frenzy late in an adulterous affair, this "Queen of Sleep" welcomes being a "thing," the safety of inner paralysis. Her beauty puts her at "the center of the world" and, a numb little "narcissus," she shelters there behind her blank face, the pool where others see their dreams.

When she was seven, her crazed father had kidnapped her, lifting a schoolyard fence and enticing her away; and people continue to do with her what they will until, after a breakdown, she leaves her muscular, meaty-breathed husband—a lawyer who pushes "more deeply into certain people than they were in their own souls"—and seeks out her ex-lover, another energetic lawyer, now frightened of her, who has just adopted a son to save his marriage. All the better that he recoils from her! It makes him more of a prize. "Never in her life had she conquered any territory, achieved any victories." But now "she would cross over into adulthood to get him, into the excitement of evil." Feeling "the elation of risk," she lifts up the fence, experimental, enticing. . . .

As Oates has been showing sympathy to mysticism in her essays, so Elena is drawn to Mered Dawe, a radical, saintly advocate of "light love," which lifts "us up into the galaxy." "Dream me," she pleads. But, no, he has "come too soon in history." Like Elena herself, he is trapped in the middle world between mineral peace and spiritual transcendence—the world of "ordinary loving maulings, or beatings and legal imprisonment," which "cannot be escaped." And, in truth, once Elena inhabits her body, "every part of it," and realizes "that everything is awake, the universe is awake," she prefers this squalid middle world of "energy," with its "gloating, greedy need." She *will* not "be solved."

So it is that, though Oates's world is scarcely less raw and terrible than before, the lighting has changed, and what was hell has become a heroic arena, where we "fight one another, compete from birth till death." No longer nihilistic, a nightmarish cat's paw—teasing, destructive—it is now freely Nietzschean, elatedly frictional, its horizons steaming with spoils. In *Do with Me What You Will*, which turns like a talon on its title, "kinship" is the mutual respect of enemy warriors—the man Elena goes out to conquer has a "backbone . . . like a whip." Even more than in Lawrence, the air is electric. "It was crude and jarring, the way people registered other people. There was something violent in it, criminal, murderous. But it was exciting also, a kind of ceaseless swirl of consciousness, currents of thought, of desire"; to such lion-mouthed challenges the novel almost unwittingly throws its liberal and mystical ideas.

The optimism this book brings to Oates's sharply contracted sense of life enlarges it only by allowing it the air of the future, the feat of time. To read Oates is still to feel all but reduced to a hungry mouth. Like Ted Hughes and certain other contemporary writers, she occupies the inner fastness of biology as a last stand against death. Egocentrism is her bow, her quiver. She wants the sensation of living to flare so high that it will send the terrors back into the night. Her turbulent pages make no apology for virtual annihilation of Western moral culture; indeed, most seem unaware of it.

As a novelist Oates succeeds through her hypnotic dramatization of the "single cell"—through a hallucinatory effect of imaginative necessity. At her best she commands you, seals you off from everything else. And in *Do with Me What You Will* she is, as often as not, at her best. Like its immediate predecessors, *them* and *Wonderland*, the book is abstract in style, abrasively concrete in subject, striking in its relentless and subtle pursuit of psychological observation, perfunctory in presenting some of the characters (Elena's husband and, except for his radiantly sick letters from prison, Mered Dawe), exciting in the freedom it invents for the others, cautiously original in technique, and boldly indifferent to formal intentness or intricate netting while propelled forward by successive new impetuses, in the jagged rhythm of life.

In trusting to this rhythm, however, Oates's books grow slightly dim in the intervals between compulsive actions. Moreover, somewhat muffled by its Sleeping Beauty. *Do with Me What You Will* has fewer strong climaxes than *them* and *Wonderland* and perhaps less of the hum of immediate duration. On the other hand, it begins and ends better and, even though the chief characters are hard to care about until the close, reads itself rather eagerly. You open it only to go on, held wondering by one of the most formidable talents of the age.

GORDON O. TAYLOR

Joyce Carol Oates,
Artist in Wonderland

"Now I am in a state of spiritual exhaustion, I think, from the last novel I did, *Wonderland*, a novel about brains—the human brain—which was my most ambitious novel and almost did me in," states Joyce Carol Oates, in an interview by mail for the February 1972 *Atlantic Monthly*. An unexceptional statement, to be expected in the wake of intense imaginative effort. Yet the public impression (whatever the private reality) of her career thus far is one of such uninterrupted fluency of creation that her suggestion here of having been brought to an "exhausted" halt strikes one as singular. It *seems* as if she had never had occasion to say that before, and therefore still less now to say that *Wonderland* "might be my last novel, at least my last large, ambitious novel."

There will surely be other large and ambitious novels by Joyce Carol Oates. Simultaneous with her expression of imaginative depletion in the *Atlantic* is her announcement of a forthcoming book of stories, now published as *Marriages and Infidelities*. And a new novel, *Do with Me What You Will*, has been recently published. But even as a fiction in its own right, a self-characterization, her sense of impasse in the aftermath of *Wonderland* informs our approach to the novel. It prompts us to ask how the book can seem at once a culmination and a termination, a "way through" and a cul-de-sac in the terrain of Miss Oates's art. So also the novel's hero—Jesse Harte/Pedersen/Vogel, in whose successive names are invested at least as many selves—seeks in the configurations of the human

From *The Southern Review* 10, no. 2 (April 1974). © 1974 by Louisiana State University.

brain (he becomes a neurosurgeon) a way through to completed, and thus liberated, personality. Yet by inwardly tightening circles of mental experience, he finds within his own confining skull the absolute truth in the form of an absolute trap.

The general structure of *Wonderland* is also inwardly spiraling, shell-like. Late in the story Jesse's daughter, Michele, is metamorphosed to "Shelley" and finally to "Shell," the spark of her life dying deep within herself, her outward self awash among millions of shells on a Florida beach suddenly prehistoric, the pelicans like pterodactyls, "giant birds . . . with terrible beaks." She is elsewhere imagined as becoming invertebrate and contracting back, "dreaming back," to the protective imprisonment of a single cell, or as ceasing to exist except as a thought in Jesse's mind, needing only to be forgotten to be free. Similar contractions or inwindings of consciousness occur in Jesse's mind. For everyone in *Wonderland* the present is a pressure gauge of an accumulating past; for each of them *"the past is always there, in your head."* So too the narrative space of the novel, like cellular space or the chambers of a shell, is curved. It bears in through its division into three "books" toward a terminus in Jesse's baffled brain, in a last encounter with his daughter filled with the exhaustion and the energy of nightmare. This final scene also, like the innermost chamber of a nautilus, seems to flow back into the shell's outer structure, returns us to the novel's beginning where a sequence from it is set as if in epigraph alongside formal epigraphs from Borges and Yeats.

We might even think of the whole body of Miss Oates's fiction as tending inward toward (and circling out again from?) *Wonderland*, rather than as a linear development. The book might then stand at the center of the record of her imaginative life, a pressure gauge of an accumulating artistic past, her explosive prolificness in reality an implosive intensification. Or, to borrow one of her recurring images, this novel would be the iris to the eye of her vision as a novelist. (The poem "Wonderland" which prefaces the novel, ascribed to a character, was first published by Miss Oates as "Iris into Eye.") It would thus not be a question of her feeling "written out" by the effort of *Wonderland* so much as one of her having written herself *into* a condition in which the novel's images seem as ineradicable from her consciousness as those which obsess her protagonist. She writes in the *Atlantic* interview:

> Any study of the human brain leads one again and again to the most despairing, unanswerable questions . . . there is no way out of the physical fact of the brain, no way *out* of this confine-

ment. . . . It has been months since I've finished *Wonderland*, but I can't seem to get free of it. I keep reliving parts of it.

"The family chronicle is Joyce Carol Oates's chosen form," said Robert M. Adams in reviewing *them*, a remark more accurate than her frequent consignment to "the fictional museum of the grotesque." Miss Oates speaks in the *Atlantic* of the family as a universe in itself from which "there's no escape. . . . And if something has gone wrong inside this small universe, then nothing can ever be made right." Something goes wrong, to say the least, in Jesse Harte's universe at the outset of *Wonderland*: his father slaughters wife and unborn baby, three children, and then himself, having wounded Jesse, who alone escapes to live—and tell through reliving—the tale. (Like Ishmael indeed, Jesse contains within his mind the mainspring-in-reverse of Miss Oates's narrative line, driven not by its uncoiling but by its tightening toward the point at which it must, like Jesse himself, either break or release and relive itself once more.) Thus, at fourteen, Jesse survives the first of several obliterations of himself, liberations from the past which yet fix the images and deposit the weight of the past inescapably in his brain. The shotgun's roar becomes as it recedes an echoing darkness out of which, for him, the universe must be re-created. New possibilities abound, but each is marked by what it can no longer be. The family chronicle, suddenly obviated, must be a chronicle of search for renewed family and self, circular and reenactive rather than traditionally sequential in form.

Book 1, *variations on an american hymn*, carries Jesse from his orphaning in 1939 in an upstate New York village through brief periods on his grandfather's farm, in an orphanage, and as the adopted son of Dr. Pedersen of Lockport—first of three surrogate fathers from the medical world in whom brilliance is imbued with madness. The section ends with an "eradicating" note from Pedersen to Jesse, pronouncing him dead to the family for a betrayal of family trust. The "facts" of Jesse's experience during this time matter less, however, than the textures and tonalities of his awareness. These *are* the facts in which Miss Oates is interested, the notes in which she composes her "variations." (She too hears America singing, but not, a century later, in Whitman's hymnal tones.)

Even before the massacre, Jesse's thought suggests a tenuousness of connection to reality that is a resource for survival in a world the reality of which is open to the novel's questioning. Borges states in Miss Oates's epigraph from *Labyrinths*:

We . . . have dreamt the world. We have dreamt it as firm, mysterious, visible, ubiquitous in space and durable in time; but

in its architecture we have allowed tenuous and eternal crevices
of unreason which tell us it is false.

So Jesse sees in the "spider web of cracks" in a ceiling the "frail formal
pattern that dreams suggest," the emptiness of the cracks becoming the
expression of substance and form. Like molecular interstices, proportionally
vast, such fissures are everywhere beneath the surfaces of life through which
Jesse sometimes slips into void. Being driven homeward by his father toward his intended death, he feels himself absorbed into the "empty white
cold" of a snow-filled sky, a "dimension of fog and space, like the future
itself." It is also at moments a dimension of ice, his vision arrested and the
world dissolved by the delicate tracings on frost-coated windows, similar in
fragility and ambiguous power over the aspect of reality to the traceries of
brain tissue which later fascinate him. His instinct for danger is felt as frozen
silence about to burst into splinters of light and sound. He throws himself
through a window to escape his father, the shatter of glass and the noise of
shots coalescing with the blankness into which he runs, "against the wall of
snow— . . . into the dark."

He recovers from his physical wounds on his grandfather's farm, submerged within himself as if unborn. The iron hardness of winter sky and
earth "matched something in himself"; one thinks (and will again) of the
cold, locked intensities of Faulkner's Joe Christmas, another figure veering
toward impasse in pursuit of his own phantasmagoric personality. Jesse and
his grandfather are "together in their silence, flowing the same way with the
passage of each day, time itself a tangible element that carried them forward, always forward, away from the past." One thinks (and already has)
of Huckleberry Finn and the healing suspensions of the river. Miss Oates is
at times playing variations on American literary hymns.

Refuge and reality are at this point the same for Jesse, both concen-
trated in the sheer functioning of his body, "the pounding of his blood . . .
that pronounced his name for him." But his grandfather breaks their com-
pact of silence, and Jesse is thrust back up through the surface of his dark
interior pool. He leaves the farm, makes his way back to his now empty
home, sits through the night as if inside the broken skull of the Jesse who
had been meant to die there, reentered through the random "design" of
shadows on shot-scarred walls upon both his future and his past. And still
his pulse affirms, "*Jesse Harte is here, a survivor.*"

Survival, however, is also metamorphosis in *Wonderland*, a chrysalid
pressure from which Jesse will never be free. One survives inward as much
as forward in this novel, the past an enclosing accretion out of which the

forms of the future emerge and into which they are reabsorbed. As Jesse's later interests converge on the brain, as its structures and pathologies become the metaphors of his own obsessions, the audible "triumph" of his heartbeat, proclaiming his personal reality, fades into the silently flickering mystery of brain function. Electroencephalographic displays, clinical verifications of life, become in Jesse's broodings representations of his own unreality: ghostly signals from a mind caught in the past, from a consciousness which has survived its own annihilation by electrochemical explanation of its processes. So in *Expensive People*, Miss Oates's narrator likens family photographs taken before he was born, which therefore annihilate him, to the light of stars which no longer exist, pure representation of a universe which may long since have exploded or dissolved.

Metamorphic "becoming," a dissolution as well as a development of self, is thus established as the major theme of *Wonderland*. One thinks back to the author's note in which the language of a conventional disclaimer produces a subtly different effect. Characters, events, and settings are not so much stated to be fictional and therefore not to be confused with real counterparts, as they are suggested to be representations of the confusions between real and unreal which exist in both life and art. When Miss Oates says, "any resemblance to reality is accidental and should be resisted," she elaborates the point. Between real and unreal lies not a separating seam, the notion of which the reader must resist, but a collision point, the "point x" in some of her stories, the point at which psychic accidents occur. Thus, she builds a dimension of literary theory into her subject in *Wonderland*, the novel itself perhaps a metamorphic event in her literary career. She writes in the author's note to *them*, of a former student's life story which provided the basis for a central characterization: "My initial feeling about her life was, 'This must be fiction, this can't all be real!' My more permanent feeling was, 'This is the only kind of fiction that is real.' " So too, in certain stories, characters feel themselves caught *as* "characters" in "fictions" which are the realities of their own lives. So indeed, the narrator of *Expensive People*, moving toward "point x" in the cross hairs of his sniperscope, theorizes on the differences between the novel he inhabits and his own mad "memoir," which are one and the same.

The "becoming" of Jesse Pedersen further dramatizes this concept of metamorphosis. Welcomed into the Pedersen family, yet absorbed as well into its extreme pathologies, Jesse experiences the release of ambition and ability while constantly exposed to confusions between the normal and the pathological. Whatever there is to be in his later life of ordered and stable purpose is partly rooted in this period. Thus, new hairline cracks of unreality are etched into these emerging structures of self. Images embodying such interfusions accumulate like coral toward formation of an interior condition, paradoxically firm like the skeletal debris on which the living coral builds, which Alfred Kazin has ascribed to the novelist herself: "She is attached to life by well-founded apprehensions that nothing lasts, nothing is safe, nothing is all around us." The important thing about the statement, as the shifted emphasis in its final clause implies, is that this *is* a form of attachment to life, and therefore a form of procedure in art.

Through Pedersen, Jesse becomes aware of the invisible world of the body, its processes mysterious and remote in the microscopic view, like galactic phenomena in the telescopic. Cellular process is the principle of the future Pedersen envisions, a model he distorts just as cancer distorts normal cell growth. Enormously fat (Jesse too begins to bloat, his outgrown clothes like sloughed skins), Pedersen proclaims all life a "movement into the infinite . . . or it is a shrinking back. Make up your mind" (though the "mind," according to his own metaphor, is "made up" as much in the genetic code as by any conscious act). History is for him the voice of death rather than a force behind life (though this conflicts with the body's biochemical "history" as a force for its future). The death of God has left a void into which the human brain, itself now the sum and substance of human freedom (though each of its cells is thus also a prison cell), may self-creatively (or self-destructively) expand. As the parentheses suggest, each of these notions lies close to its contradiction; each positive image is shadowed by its photographic negative. Pedersen's definition of life slips over into evocation of malignancy, his own life a cancerous re-creation of itself in negative terms, his presumption "to become God" a redefinition of God as the ultimate Carcinogen.

Jesse is baffled by all this, and to the reader Pedersen is more absurd than appalling. This sequence comes closer than any in the novel to black comedy, a mode Miss Oates has disparaged as "consistently allowing most readers to dissociate themselves from what they are reading." "Trick" Monk, a character who more knowingly insists on the malignancies of being, later confronts Jesse with a vision at once more abhorrent and less easily dismissed. Nevertheless, with Pedersen's words echoing in his skull—"*A human being . . . must become what he was meant to be*"—Jesse senses the empty fatality of nonmeaning nonbeing behind them, glimpses their photonegative antireality, which to him is "something invisible and terrifying in its reality." And in disowning Jesse, Pedersen declares: "You have no existence. You are nothing." Thus, Jesse survives himself once more, his "death" as Jesse Pedersen a "seamless" entry into life as Jesse Vogel—

his grandfather's name—another loop from the past on the loom of the future.

The years of medical training in Ann Arbor and Chicago "were to break into a few sharp images for him," and the novel's two remaining books increasingly consist of mental images broken and reblended by exchanges of pressure between present and past, real and unreal. Like glacial ice, Jesse's consciousness is subject both to fracture and flow, its images continually realigned by compressions of memory, its progress a self-entrapment within narrowing rock walls of its own carving. As Jesse inadvertently conceives it, and as Miss Oates then relates it to her own method, his story is increasingly composed of fragments making up the whole, but experienced or dealt with artistically *as* fragments. Swiftly able to absorb medical texts, Jesse encounters a curious resistance in fiction:

> He was unable to follow a plot. He was unable to see the careful evolution of a story. The necessary pattern, the rhythm that demanded completion, the internal heat, the gravity that forced everything to a suitable conclusion . . . what did all these things mean? . . . He had the idea that what people thought were stories were fragments from shattered wholes, the patterns, the brain waves, of a certain man at a certain time in his life . . . therefore all writing was autobiography, wasn't it? His instructor, an earnest young New Yorker, had tried to explain what was wrong with Jesse's ideas.

Jesse's notion of a novel is not Miss Oates's, though along with the "earnest young New Yorker's" it may comprise her double image of this novel's necessary form. (A writer who teaches, a New Yorker who has taught in Michigan, Miss Oates sometimes conspires or contends with herself on such questions in her own fiction.) *Wonderland* is a composed whole, though not necessarily therefore wholly stable. It contains the rhythm demanding completion, generates the internal heat, the gravity forcing a conclusion, but it poises rather than resolves these energies and only for the representational moment. Homeostasis, figuring in the story as a physiological process, perhaps also figures as an artistic principle: equilibrium and unity maintained by interplay among tendencies toward instability and fragmentation. In fragmentation thus *is* structure, a "frail formal pattern" to the novel itself like spidery cracks in a ceiling, fissures in glacial flow, or branchings of coral in the sea.

Jesse moves successfully ahead in his career, metamorphosed again by the loss of his Pedersen fat, driven by a sense of nearness at last to the safety

of a "completed" future. Yet even while "forcing his future into place"—
marrying, fathering children, advancing in his specialty—he remains haunted
and the narrative dominated by images deflecting inward his forward pro-
jections, back-eddies in the flow of consciousness and time:

> There were other parts of his brain, dim and insoluble, unfathom-
> able, where other Jesses existed, sinister and unkillable. . . . If he
> could have snipped certain neural pathways in his brain blood-
> lessly, he would have done it . . . but it was impossible. He would
> always live inside himself.

In dreams, or in waking moments of panic, he feels himself slipping into
different dimensions. Sometimes he is "skimming back across the miles of
road to that house, that intersection of roads" where his family died, just as
in other Oates stories people rush toward "point x" or trace their entrap-
ments on freeways, misnamed neural pathways of urban life. Sometimes he
is awash in the social mass, in historical, even cosmic, flux: "Time was
mobbed with people. How could he establish himself, construct himself, in
such a mob . . . ?" In personal relationships too, pursuing self-construction,
Jesse experiences a dispersion of self. Even together with his wife he is lost
to himself as well as to her, their love-"making" a dissolution into silence,
the unreality of their separate dreams the mirror-reality of their marriage.
He senses the infusion by his mentors rather than the growth within himself
of his professional skill. First Dr. Cady, whose daughter, Helene, Jesse
marries, then Dr. Perrault, whose protégé he becomes—fathers and abandon-
ers of Jesse in their turn—seem able, like Pedersen and Jesse's true father
before them, to invade his being, to "stare into the hollow spaces of his
skull."

To Cady, human beings are "perfect machines" who fear the idea of
biochemical mechanism because they cannot understand the mechanical
base of their existence. Yet words such as "*destiny, beauty*" shimmer on the
edges of his scientific understanding; he too has seen the universe in the
structures and spaces revealed by the microscope. And he too fears to follow
as Perrault's research pushes deeper into the brain's recesses. For Perrault,
however, "there was nothing to fear": "the human brain was not sacred . . .
it was touchable. It was matter." Like some Ahab survived and grown old,
bleached of passion and drily content with the blanknesses behind the masks,
Perrault reenacts his triumph daily in surgery. His universe has shrunk to
the contours of the human skull, his "inviolable" operating room like a
violated chamber of the brain, even his offices skull-like—"He peered out of
[their] sinister whiteness as if out of a cave flooded with light." He too lives

locked within his own mind, as he later dies there of a ruptured vessel in the brain, victim to what he had claimed to control. Jesse had set out to "copy the man," to *be* Perrault, or perhaps had been chosen by Perrault for that purpose. Thirteen years after Perrault's death, still sensing the old man's presence in his brain, Jesse completes a book left unfinished by Perrault and in composing a preface suggests the extent to which surviving him entails sharing in his death; sharing too in the death-in-life of Perrault's final outlook:

> All of us who knew Dr. Perrault have been shaped by him and
> we will never outlive him. We will never outlive outlive outlive
> his death death death
The last sentence trailed away.

Jesse's wife, Helene, also comes to know the precariousness of her own reality and veers violently toward the edge of impossibility. Pregnant with their first child, she broods on the physical metamorphoses involved, generating thoughts of still more threatening transformations. A microscope slide idly glimpsed becomes a simultaneous image of cosmic and fetal creation, poised on the moment of nonbeing just prior to actual formation— her own being lost in the image's distances. The crumbling of a half-razed building, pipes and wires "like exposed nerves," becomes a strange, negative version of the "explosion of small, soft, gentle cells" within her. Never before aware of her body, she senses its historicity—"layer upon layer the years had formed her" (again like coral formation), and now the metamorphic layerings pressure her as closely as the new tissues within; past and future fusing in a precarious present moment. Awaiting examination in a doctor's office, a magnified photograph of a cell dizzies her at the thought that "she herself . . . was made up of such cells and nothing else." It seems to her that the "universe might open up into a snowstorm of cells." The closing image of Joyce's "The Dead," the swoon of Gabriel's soul into the snowy death of his dreams, here becomes a more violent "opening up into" the life of nightmare, in which the constructions and dissolutions of being are conjoined. The encounter with nullity is as numbing as Forster's Mrs. Moore's in the Marabar Caves; Helene feels herself in, and in herself, a "vacuum."

Also extraordinary are the sequences involving Reva Denk, unsubtly named but subtly rendered as a figure half in and half out of the novel's objective reality. Characterized entirely through Jesse's fantasies, she still must be dealt with in terms of plot. The reader "knows" but cannot prove, anymore than Jesse can later remember, precisely when she first appears in an emergency ward, her *dis*appearance from which is the more telling sign of her dramatic existence. She too is a metamorphic being, and like Jesse she has other names, each a fragment of the mirror in which she can therefore never be wholly reflected. In his visions of her she promises reality and life, yet the vision she offers to him is one of raw chaos and death. He rejects it, as eventually he rejects her. But, as with Helene, the nullifying image lasts. The disintegrative vision becomes still more his own as he searches decaying areas of Chicago and Toronto for his runaway daughter, adrift herself in a dim wonderland of drugs, pursuing self-"erasure."

Wonderland's short concluding book, *dreaming america*, moves freely in time through the determinations of memory, its psychological and textual fragmentations drawing energy from their reachings toward (never into) homeostatic repose. Looping back and thrusting forward, the narrative accelerates through the sixties toward 1971, the "present" of the novel's compositional completion as well as of its final scenes. Jesse's accumulated past also rushes toward collision with his present; the wheel comes full circle and he is there, no prospect now for Shakespearean regeneration— only the final coilings of the inward psychic spiral. He feels himself coming "to the end of himself," his life "subsiding" like lines receding in perspective to a single street, a single doorway where he finds Michele. Just as his wife is drawn into the vortex of his isolation and feels herself annihilated there, so his daughter, long drowning in the pool of his mind, is dying at last in the ebb of her own.

History itself seems to Jesse to be crumbling even as it accelerates, collapsing inward with John Kennedy's skull in 1963, its lines of force dissolving into television shadows throughout the decade. Now arrived at his own phantasmal sense of being what Pedersen had proclaimed himself— "a citizen of the twentieth century"—Jesse writes in a professional article of clinical data which seem, by their setting in Miss Oates's narrative, as much a theory of history as an unconscious insight into his own case history:

> It seems that events of the distant past are more firmly estab-
> lished in the memory, with no regard to their relative (conscious)
> significance or insignificance to the individual; current and re-
> cent events are precarious and may be extinguished completely
> by traumatic injury. . . . Brain damage may result in the extinc-
> tion of all memory, of course, but it seems that the mere organic
> existence of the brain assures a constantly-strengthening foun-
> dation of distant memories.

Increasingly thus isolated from time itself as well as from the unreal reality of the times, from family, and from self, Jesse experiences a mental version of the cul-de-sac in his own father's brain, out of which the novel itself initially explodes:

> Better to give up, erase them all, destroy them, obliterate them and the memory of them, wipe everything out. A father could wipe out everything he had ever done and be free. A clean, pure, empty being, a void.

Novel-ending violence in *Light in August*, at once liberating and annihilating Joe Christmas, becomes in *Wonderland* the novel-launching violence from which winds the double helix of Jesse's annihilation and survival—a survival without liberation. For Jesse knows at the end, as if in echo or anticipation of Miss Oates's words in *The Edge of Impossibility* (a study of tragic forms published next after *Wonderland*), that "being is an empty fiction, and our 'becoming' is equally fictitious, equally empty." Like Shelley on her ancient beach in Florida, a shell among shells, he knows "how many more dead there were than living, how deeply the earth was filled with the fine siftings of their bones!"

Dreaming america also intensifies and reinfuses into *Wonderland* as a whole a reader's sense of what Miss Oates's *Atlantic* interviewer calls an "atmosphere of autobiographical confusion, that is, of the mixture of fiction with details that suggested some autobiographical accuracy." One sees again, as in the author's note, an emphasis on mergings rather than relationships between facts and fictions. The topicalities of this last section are drawn into the region where real frays into unreal, the novel's true psychological terrain, rather than allowed to provide anchors or escape routes to the "normal." But one senses a more personal meaning for "autobiographical confusion," an internalized urgency of "accurate" response to conditions, more than a concern with recognizable "details." It may be worth noting that in both *them* and *Wonderland* Miss Oates picks up the life stories of her protagonists in approximately the year of her own birth, 1938, though the characters themselves are born earlier. As each novel drives toward conclusion in what is nearly the present moment for the novelist herself as she completes the book, this sense of autobiographical urgency, of personal response to the converging forces and pressuring atmosphere of the times, increases. It is as if entering the histories of her characters at the point and in the way she does were a way of reentering and retracing herself; a way (to quote her own prefatory poem despite its fictional ascription) of

> *entering my own history like a tear*
> *balanced on the outermost edge*
> *of the eyelid*

In that tear are both her commitment to reality and her journey through the looking glass.

G. F. WALLER

Joyce Carol Oates's Wonderland: *An Introduction*

> When Aristotle notes that man is a
> rational animal one strains
> forward, cupping his ear, to hear which
> of those words is emphasized.
> —*Expensive People*

Despite constant praise from reviewers, the writings of Joyce Carol Oates have so far attracted little detailed critical commentary. Her productivity, certainly, has been widely noted: in ten years, she has published some six novels, including the award-winning *them,* four collections of stories, four volumes of poems, a book of critical essays, as well as many uncollected reviews, essays, and poems. Already, this list will undoubtedly be out of date—a checklist of her works published in *American Literature* in 1971 is now dramatically dated, and even then had omitted many items. Such prolific productivity by a writer who, in addition, is a full-time professor of literature at the University of Windsor, might suggest an obsession with words, and even imply a lack of self-criticism in her writing. Certainly, her books reveal an enviable fluency that often overflows into carelessness, inadequate characterization, or arbitrary structure. But her verbal profligacy is offset by some of the most compelling writing in contemporary fiction—in particular, she possesses a peculiarly chilling ability to evoke some of the darker recesses of the contemporary sensibility, to penetrate our fears and insecurities and the deep-seated threats to our sense of personal and communal identity. In what follows, I hope to initiate some analysis of

From *The Dalhousie Review* 54, no. 3 (Autumn 1974). © 1974 by Dalhousie University Press.

a writer who is arguably one of the most important novelists in North America—and, specifically since her migration from Detroit to Windsor in 1967, in Canada.

Miss Oates's fundamental subjects are most clearly, if sometimes superficially, seen in her short stories: she is insistently concerned with the fragility of the human personality in contemporary America, and with examining the threatening undercurrent of violence ever present just beneath the serene surface of suburban living. Many of her stories, however, give the impression of being written at white heat, thrown off as one insight after another seizes her. Their clarity of expression, as opposed to their vision, frequently falters. Some, certainly, are masterpieces: at times she has a frighteningly clear insight into, say, the felt terror of poverty in the city, or the obsessive grasping and destructiveness of a collapsing marriage, or the velvet-gloved ruthlessness of strife between generations. "Plot," for instance, evokes in a gripping manner what the woman narrator describes as the "peculiar boredom in her glands. Women have that boredom today." (*Marriages and Infidelities*). Similarly, in "Scenes of Passion and Despair" the narrator broods on her husband and her lover in a passage very typical of Miss Oates's insight into characters living in a volatile state of half-courage and fear:

> If his drinking got too bad and he really got sick, she would abandon her lover and nurse him. If he killed himself she would abandon her lover and wear black. Years of mourning. Guilt. Sin. If he found out about her lover and ran over and killed him, shot him right in that bed, she would wear black, she would not give evidence against him, she would come haggard to court, a faithful wife again.
>
> The husband will not get sick, will not kill himself, will not kill the lover or even find out about him; he will only grow old.
>
> She will not need to wear black or to be faithful; she will grow old.
>
> The lover will not even grow old: he will explode into molecules as into a mythology.
>
> (*Marriages and Infidelities*)

In the novels, the obsessions, despair, paradoxes, and fears that characterize Oates's stories are welded more satisfactorily into a peculiarly gothic structure, its gargoyles and extravagances growing compellingly out of the everyday paraphernalia of contemporary social realities. The settings of the novels have affinities with the broad naturalistic tradition of Flaubert, Crane,

Dreiser, even Faulkner. They range from the itinerant fruitpickers of South Carolina, the urban poor and affluent professionals of Detroit, to the University, the medical research clinic, and above all the spiritual tundra of North American suburbia, where even the rules of society are appropriately broken "in an orderly way" (*Expensive People*). Through these apparently ordinary settings frequently erupt the latent terror, violence, obsessive sexuality, religious strife Oates perceives lying close to the surface of contemporary life. Her novels are thus not really related to the naturalistic tradition, but are more in the tradition of American Gothic, with sudden upsurges of violence or unexpected lyricism, exploding through day-to-day surface. Richard, the grotesque 250 pound eighteen-year-old who narrates *Expensive People,* describes his own environment, which is typical of most of her novels: "Fernwood, and Brookfield and Cedar Grove and Charlotte Pointe," all redolent with the odor of cash, with the Johns Behemoth private school, the Vastvalley Country Club, the constantly aspiring and mobile professional caste. Such a setting is related to what she describes, in the novel of the same name, as "Wonderland," with its symbolic structures of supermarkets, "decorated with 'modern' multicolored cubes and benches of garish carnival colors," the ersatz of amplified music, "square after square of cubes and benches and potted plants." In *Expensive People,* the equivalent to "Wonderland" is called, ironically, "Paradise."

From such familiar surroundings, Oates builds up an impressive symbolic structure. The basic materialistic surroundings of contemporary affluence—supermarkets, consumables, money, cleanliness, success, marriage, motherhood—are all heightened into the material of Gothic parable. Wonderland is revealed as Wasteland: surrounding themselves with the paraphernalia and the superficialities of affluence, modern Americans are still guiltily aware of an inner darkness their neon and strobe lighting barely illuminate.

Wonderland is a society of schizoids: its inhabitants define their goals in the rhetoric of idealism—the integrity of the individual, the promise of the future, the freedom and uniqueness of the personality—but it acts as if these great goals of the Renaissance and Enlightenment, Bruno's or Nietzsche's dreams of human autonomy, are graspable only in the most immediate material forms. The constant pressure to growth, to discovery, is defined in idealistic terms—"life is a movement into the infinite . . . or it is a shrinking back"—but it is experienced only in terms of economics, ego-expression, exploitation. The struggle to assert one's individuality ends, as with Macbeth, in being subject to the terrifying determinism of constant material competition and destruction. So Jesse, the hero of *Wonderland,*

finds that in "forcing his future into place," his contemporaries and surroundings, his present (as opposed to his future) are all experienced as
threats. Frustration and insecurity, Oates suggests, are not merely urged
upon us by the consumer society, which conditions us to crave more, newer,
bigger consumables; more fundamentally, they are at the very root of our
contemporary consciousness and result not just in our physical dissatisfac-
tions, but in the destruction of the very autonomy we strive for. Grasping
for the freedom of the supermarket, we become more and more subject to
its demands. Striving for autonomy, Jesse finds "even his spirit was become
automated, mechanized. It worked perfectly for him. He had only to direct
it and it responded."

Them won for Miss Oates the National Book Award for 1970, but
Wonderland is probably her most completely realised novel, and deserves a
wide audience and careful critical attention. It is central to her vision of
America, using as its primary symbols money, food and eating, cleanliness,
the struggle for success and social respectability—and, beneath these
surface manifestations of contemporary affluence, violence. *Wonderland*
relates the history of Jesse—successively Harte, Vogel, Pedersen, Vogel.
Jesse is orphaned when his bankrupt father shoots the rest of his family and
himself, and is brought up, educated and so formed by, first, his
grandfather, then a Boys Home, the brilliant Doctor Pedersen, the
University of Chicago, Postgraduate Medical School, from which he
progresses to his final environment, his marriage, wife, and children.
Through all these rapidly changing environments and experiences, Jesse
constantly fights to discover and develop his inner personality. Moulded by
radically dissociated influences, continually under pressure to achieve
status, stability, relatedness, he needs a sense of his own identity.
Otherwise, each successive experience is "all a blur, shapeless, a dimension
of fog and space, like the future itself."

What does, in its sinister pervasiveness, link Jesse's successive worlds,
is money. It is the lack of money that drives his father to murder and suicide.
As his father drives him home from school for the last time, the display
window of Montgomery Ward's, with its "galaxy of gifts" is a threatening
mixture of temptation:

> There is a village you can buy, tiny cardboard houses on a white
> board, with a church at its center. Jesse's mother wanted one of
> these but they were too expensive. Everything is too expensive
> this year. Last year. The year before that: everything too expen-
> sive. They have no money. . . . He wants a shotgun but there is

no chance of getting it. No, no chance. There is no money. . . .
Who can afford such things. Where are the people who can
afford such things?

With the Pedersens, Jesse discovers the answer. But he also discovers the
destructiveness of having money. The Pedersens, "with their soft,
gelatinous bodies," are a horrifying caricature of affluent consumers. They
are all gross, stuffed, "like pale sausages" yet possessing nevertheless, a
religion of rarefied spiritualism. The Pedersens epitomise the society's
collective schizophrenia, between the rhetoric of spirituality and the
materialism of their actions. Eating becomes a sacred act, an obscene
mock-Eucharist:

> The lips parted, the mouth opened, something was inserted into
> the opening, then the jaws began their centuries of instinct, raw
> instinct, and the food was moistened, ground into pulp, swal-
> lowed. It was magic . . . Hilda watched her father covertly and
> saw how his nostrils flared with the exertion of eating, his face
> slowly reddened, a handsome face, sharply handsome inside that
> pouched, bloated encasement of skin, his eyes sharp and glisten-
> ing as the eyes of skinny, devilish birds.

The greed of the Pedersens reveals not just a waste of resources, but a
destruction of personality. Similarly with that allied fetish of the American
way of life, cleanliness. B.O. was not discovered by Americans for nothing:
fixed to the ultimate and sole reality of the material, Americans have tried
to scrub, cauterize, deodorize, perfume the body, in a frenetic attempt to
have it assume the role of the spirit that they have, in reality, abandoned.
Jesse finds himself "contagious"; he obsessively washes; he "remembered
with disapproval the years of his life he had been dirty, his hands crawling
with germs. Now he understood how the invisible world of germs ruled the
visible world, how there were friendly bacteria and unfriendly bacteria, and
how it was necessary to control them as much as possible." Again, behind
the obsessive materialism lies the vocabulary of the spiritual, as the bacteria
become the good and bad angels of the contemporary world. Oates's ob-
servations on the fetishes of our world are, of course, not especially original;
but she uses them as starting points to analyse the ways the concept of
personality may be cheapened, distorted, or shattered. Such a concentration
on money, food, and hygiene represent a fantasy world foisted upon us by
the ad-mass society, giving us apparently tantalisingly easy access to just
those products and experiences which seem most easily to fulfil our desires,

make us more beautiful, admirable, free. Their very ease of access is at once a distortion of personality and an invitation by which we are led to believe in the absoluteness of the glittering surface of Wonderland.

The novel's most insistent concern, therefore, becomes the nature of the human personality—and on this subject Oates becomes more than just a penetrating commentator on the all too observable drives of contemporary life. Like John Updike's anatomy of New England suburbia, *Wonderland* offers a parable of the condition of twentieth-century man. Unlike Updike— with whom, however, she has certain stylistic affinities—she has no theo- logical *parti pris*, no nostalgic harking back to the specific ideals of the founding fathers. A lapsed Catholic, her frame of reference is grounded in Christianity, but her real affinities are with Sartre and Heidegger. What seems to be her main philosophical target is, specifically, the frightening plausibility yet spiritual inadequacy of the modern phenomenological ac- count of the self.

Jesse's constant problem is to define his inner being in a society that simultaneously cultivates individualism and yet is increasingly deterministic. As a substitute for the traditional belief in a mysterious yet real inner self, Wonderland offers the apparent security of facts. Technology—another of Oates's symbols of contemporary America—offers him a way out of his fears of life's mysteries. The human brain, he muses "was not sacred. It was not sacred, it was touchable. It was matter . . . a weighable and measurable thing. Beneath the think it could be squeezed and prodded like anything else. Once dead, it was dead permanently; it was no miracle in creation. There was nothing to fear." If, as Jesse learns, "the definition of life . . . was only one of behaviour" therefore, "the personality is an illusion . . . it is just a tradition." What, then, will satisfy him is personal and professional pre- dictability—ambition, success, well-defined and achievable material goals. And the great lesson he learns is "control": "if he had control of himself, Jesse Vogel, then nothing else mattered in the universe . . . life had become predictable. He was forcing his future into place."

Jesse's obsession with material certainty, with defining himself by ex- ternals, is presented as an American paradigm, as he progresses from a poor, hardworking rural schoolboy to a famous neurosurgeon. His life is an epit- ome of the work ethic—and yet, when examined, it has been achieved not by personal dynamism operating against or using weaker forces but by a series of defensive reactions to the conditions and initiatives of others: his father's poverty, Pedersen's power and ambitions, the opinion of his pro- fessors and peers. He is essentially formed by externals. "It distressed Jesse that he must always exist in the eyes of others, their power extended in him though he did not choose them, did not choose them deliberately at all. They were a pressure on him, in his head, a pressure he loathed."

The integrated personality is, further, one that senses a continuity with an apprehended past, not one that successively inhabits disconnected worlds. In her novel, Oates is also examining the effects of discontinuity on the personality. Jesse's struggle for survival necessitates not just denying at each stage an older set of habits and surroundings, but in making a conscious attempt to create a new self—for in an obsessively materialistic world, the self becomes increasingly identified with its tangible surroundings. Thus Pedersen gives him a new name, focuses his attention not on the past but, as a scientist, on the present and the future, encouraging him to push "into the person you will be, the future that belongs to both of us." On the one hand, the human personality atrophies unless it develops; on the other, the past cannot be denied without radical distortion.

Late in the novel, Jesse's wife Helene describes to a friend how she had "found some scribbling of Jesse's . . . just pieces of scrap paper with strange designs all over, resembling human faces, and the word *homeostasis* written over and over again, maybe a hundred times." "Homeostasis" is the scientific expression of the novel's main concern, introduced to Jesse by Pedersen:

> The living being is stable. It must be so in order not to be destroyed, dissolved, or disintegrated by the colossal forces, often adverse, which surround it. By an apparent contradiction it maintains its stability only if it is excitable and capable of modifying itself according to external stimuli and adjusting its response to the stimulation. It is stable because it is modifiable— the slight instability is the necessary condition for the true stability of the organism.

Homeostasis is what the metaphysical problem of the personality has been reduced to, and for Jesse inner integrity degenerates into the fight for material stability. Outwardly successful and materially free, a surgeon with a growing reputation, inside him something essential is constricted. His control of his surroundings defines his essential being—until into his life comes Oates's constant symbol of the frightening yet often saving unpredictability of life, sexual love.

Critics of John Updike—whose affinities with Oates I briefly mentioned—have spoken of his obsession with the desperate marriage-centeredness of suburbia. Oates's best writing is similarly concerned with the tensions, betrayals, frustrations, and unpredictable joys of contemporary sexual love. As in Updike's *Couples,* in *Wonderland* sex offers man an experience simultaneously fulfilling and stable, yet alluring and unpredictable. Oates frequently uses the phrase "permanently married" to describe, usually ironically, the mixture of apparent stability and constant newness postulated in the American ideal of marriage. She is fascinated by the extent to which sex may both imprison and deliver mankind: men and women are "flesh with an insatiable soul" (*Marriages and Infidelities*), and the bond between them is equally an ambiguous and ill-definable one:

> Everywhere on this highway, at this moment, there were men and women driving together, bonded together—what did it mean to be together? What did it mean to enter into a bond with another person?
>
> (*Marriages and Infidelities*)

Into the middle of Jesse's successful career walks the unpredicted figure of Reva (suggesting "dream"), a young blonde woman to whom Jesse instinctively responds. As if embodying something in himself revolting instinctively against its repression, she reminds him, somehow, of his past. She opens up in him an aspect of himself his technological thoroughness has taught him to ignore—a mysterious depth in his personality: "somewhere," he now feels, "there were words for him, for Jesse, the exact words that would explain his life. But he did not know them. He used words shyly, crudely. It remained for someone else—a woman, perhaps—to draw these sacred words out of him, to justify him, redeem him as Jesse—he could not create them himself. Not alone." He is now caught between fear of the past she mysteriously recalls for him and excitement at the rediscovery of the unpredictable and unmeasurable aspect of the personality. In the story "The Heavy Sorrow of the Body," the narrator muses that "before falling in love, I was defined. Now I am undefined." (*The Wheel of Love*). Reva similarly brings a sense of unprepared for lack of definability into Jesse's life. So heavily conditioned by a belief in the materialism of the human personality, his spontaneity and excitement disciplined for so long, he over-reacts, plots constantly to see her, pursues her from Chicago to upstate Wisconsin, until finally, after she has promised to come away with him, he is shaving in his motel, preparing for the ultimate liberating leap into unpredictability, when he cuts himself with an unguarded razor blade:

> What if he cut himself. . . ? But he had to shave, he had no choice . . . And then lightly, timidly, he scraped the blade against his skin and blood spurted out at once.
> He stared at his own blood.

Then, again, as if hypnotized, he drew the blade against the
other side of his face.

More blood . . .

He was fascinated by the sudden streaming of blood . . . Nothing could stop it. He brought the blade down against the top of
his chest and drew it against his skin—such soft skin, shivering
beneath his touch . . .

until, finally, "He stood there, bleeding from a dozen places, unconnected
places, streaming blood so lightly, experimentally, giddily. The violence of
his past, the violence beneath the perfumed, close-shaven, cleanliness of
affluent America has surfaced. "In the end, impatiently, he decided to put
his clothes back on over the bleeding. He drove back to Chicago that way."

The novel's final book, *dreaming america,* is perhaps slightly anticlimactic, although it unfolds the next, inevitable, part in Jesse's tragedy. His
failure with Reva still haunts him uneasily, but he is now set against his
daughter, a freaked-out, drop-out, affluent teenager, representing perhaps
an inevitable reaction against Jesse's obsessive work-ethic, for whom "history is dead and anatomy is dead. Passion is the only destiny." Jesse is
obsessively drawn towards her; she reminds him of Reva and his lost glimpses
of freedom, and yet his love is a desperate possessive desire to dominate her,
to subdue and smother her with his despair. Again and again, the central
problem of homeostasis recurs: for one so conditioned by such a view of the
human organism, the deterministic mobility of America means that failure
involves death. In love with, afraid of, desiring, the freedom his daughter
has achieved, Jesse pursues her to Toronto, and there, again instinctively
returning to the destruction of his own father, he rows obsessively out along
Lake Ontario with her:

"All of you . . . everyone . . . all my life, everyone . . . Always you
are going away from me and you don't come back to explain. . . ," Jesse wept.

He embraced her. He clutched at her thighs, her emaciated
thighs, her legs. He pressed his face against her knees, weeping.

The boat drifted most of the night. Near dawn it was picked
up by a large handsome cruiser, a Royal Mounted Police boat, a
dazzling sight with its polished wood and metal and its trim of
gold and blue.

To read *Wonderland,* along with the best of Oates's other novels and
stories may be a profoundly disturbing experience. She has an admirable

ability to bring out a reader's own potential or actual neuroses, surrounded as we are by the paraphernalia of *Wonderland,* its affluence, its insistence on increasing material security, its insidious insistence on the unreality or inferiority of the past, its encouragement to us to choose the easy factuality of our surroundings rather than face the recesses of that unfathomable entity, the personality. Moreover, apart from the occasional carelessness of structure or unnecessary elaboration, the products frequently of her own obsession with words, her novels evoke their reader's responses by a dark, muscular, brooding style, as the everyday words and verbal signs erupt into deeply reverberating symbols. As John Ratti remarks, "she writes basic American English of what to the contemporary jaded eye and ear seems almost dazzling purity." A combination of compelling vision and clarity of evocation makes Joyce Carol Oates, even at thirty-five, a major figure in contemporary fiction.

EILEEN T. BENDER

Autonomy and Influence: *Joyce Carol Oates's* Marriages and Infidelities

In the realm of art, in the realm of philosophy, and in the realm which nourishes these, the realm of ordinary private experience, autonomy has proved a problematic conception. The "autonomous man" has been the culture hero of the West, striking a romantic pose, expressing the collective desire for potency and self-determination. Autonomy has been an essential indicator of self-worth. Yet growing out of this ideal, two different visions of autonomy have threatened to divide artist and philosopher. Ethical "autonomy" has seemed to predicate the supremacy of the rational intellect: the rule of reason in the sphere of morals. For the artist, however, the autonomy of art has meant an ineluctable and irresistible force which transcends and may even conflict with considerations of a moral order. Art appears to impose its own conventions, invoke its own precedents, and liberate mysterious energies beyond the artist's conscious control. To complicate the issue still further, the artist has posed as autonomous hero, struggling against limitations imposed not only by society but by art: limitations of form, and of the received artistic tradition.

Today in an age characterized by paranoia and impotence, the conception of autonomy itself has come under attack. One of its chief assailants, the behaviorist B. F. Skinner, calls for the dispossession of "autonomous man," lamenting the persistence of that anachronism. The idea of ethical autonomy seems a form of fiction, an arbitrary gesture in an irrational universe. Yet the old romance continues to play itself out, a mythic promise

From *Soundings: An Interdisciplinary Journal* 58, no. 3 (Fall 1975). © 1975 by the Society for Religion in Higher Education and the University of Tennessee.

of potency against growing odds. Like a marriage of long standing, the
covenant somehow persists in the face of numerous infidelities.

Indeed, "autonomy" is a myth with which the contemporary artist
must contend, influencing the conception of character, plot, and art itself; a
myth in the dual sense that it is widely shared and suspect. Critic Tony
Tanner provocatively describes the resulting psychodrama of American
literature:

> There is an abiding dream . . . that an unpatterned, uncondi-
> tioned life is possible, in which your movements and stillnesses,
> choices and repudiations are all your own; and . . . there is also
> an abiding American dread that someone else is patterning your
> life, that there are all sorts of invisible plots afoot to rob you of
> your autonomy of thought and action.

In many ways contemporary American literature registers the ontological insecurity born of this mixture of dream and dread. Anti-hero succeeds
hero; plot takes on devious and subversive connotations. The artist's own
autonomy—the response to tradition and convention, the struggle for originality—in many cases becomes the very subject of art. Thus Richard Poirier
describes the artist as a "performing self," striving to "keep from being
smothered by the inherited structuring of things . . . to keep within and yet
in command of the accumulations of culture that have become a part of
what he is."

Walking such a tightrope, the artist-performer is often uneasy. The
modern "fabulators"—Barth, Nabokov, Brautigan, Pynchon, Barthelme—
complain of the "someone else" patterning their art, fearing engulfment by
the inescapable literary past, calling theirs a literature of exhaustion. Defi-
antly, they offer self-conscious fictions and schemes of linguistic deception.
In another age such literature might have been labeled decadent, autono-
mist, anti-social, elitist. Today, these fabulations seem a perverse form of
realism: their self-assertions amid disturbing accounts of cosmic conspiracy
and social disorder seem to mirror the modern condition.

Joyce Carol Oates offers quite different variations on the theme of
autonomy. Paradoxically, while her fabulator-contemporaries construct
metafictions that seem all too realistic, Oates's "realism" dramatizes the
autonomous dream and dread central to the metafictive impulse. Again and
again, her work recounts the grim romance of the ego, the rage for command and control, the foredoomed struggle for self-expression. Although
she too offers arresting exhibitions of formal experiment, Oates's characteristic strategies are drawn from the literary past: she frames the interplay

of character and social force in linear narrative. Rather than resisting the inherited structuring of things, she embraces it. As she seems to contend with the myth of personal autonomy, so she seems to welcome certain limits upon art and the artist.

Like Harold Bloom, Oates sees art as derivative, as unique but not "original." For Bloom this suggests that art is "misreading" and "misalliance"; self-deception and infidelity seem art's generative energies, as the artist attempts to overcome "the anxiety of influence." For Oates, however, there is no need for extraordinary and covert resistance. Instead of perceiving literature as a series of discrete objects connected by invisible but punishing bonds, products of Oedipal anger, she describes art as open, shared discourse: "not anything permanent, frozen, or fossilized, but a way we have of humanizing one another." Oates finds her predecessors infinitely susceptible of revision and imaginative reconstruction. Artists are human personalities rather than dictators of convention. Critics then perform acts of the empathic imagination rather than feats of cartography.

Oates refuses to accept the fabulator's romantic conception of the autonomous artist-heroic isolato, radically detached from society. Contemporary literature, she claims, has become enfeebled by that ingenious but "prematurely elderly vision" of exhaustion and entropy:

> Why is it that our cleverest writers . . . have followed so eagerly the solipsistic examples of Nabokov, Beckett, and, more recently and most powerfully, Borges? Why have they never noticed that the typical works of these unique geniuses demand both the absorption of a complex, beautifully-organized library and a truly exhausted countryside? We don't have either in this country.

Oates traces the origin of this old world dream and new world nightmare to the "I"-ness of the Renaissance:

> Where at one point in civilization this very masculine, combative ideal of an "I" set against all other "I's"—and against nature as well—was necessary in order to wrench man from the hermetic contemplation of a God-centered universe and get him into action, it is no longer necessary, its health has become a pathology.

For Oates, the artist who embraces such egocentrism is doomed to "devise and defend a sealed-off universe, inhabited chiefly by the self-as-artist." Instead she suggests a radical revision of the image of the artist, a refutation of "the myth of the isolated artist," a vision of a cultural continuum of shared creative effort:

> If I were to suggest, in utter seriousness, that my fiction is the creation of thousands upon thousands of processes of consciousness, synthesized somehow in me, I would be greeted with astonishment or disbelief, or dismissed as being "too modest."

Oates charges that recognition of the communal nature of art is impossible as long as the myth of autonomy persists, a myth she finds both aesthetically and morally corrupt:

> As long as the myth of separate and competitive "selves" endures, we will have a society obsessed with adolescent ideas of being superior, of conquering, of destroying. The pronoun "I" is as much a metaphor as "schizophrenia," and it has undergone the same "metaphor-into-myth" process. Creative work, like scientific work, should be greeted as a communal effort.

Oates denies the prevalent modern view that art's energies are derived from the artist's hunger for autonomy and originality. Instead she reasserts the notion of art's own peculiar autonomy, somehow generating its own mysterious energies, working through the medium of the artist. She describes her own creative process as a relaxation of the private ego:

> My "characters" really dictate themselves to me. I am not free of them, really, and I can't force them into situations they haven't themselves willed. They have the autonomy of characters in a dream. . . . I am fascinated by people . . . and I hope my interest in them isn't vampiristic, because I don't want to take life from them, but only to honor the life in them.

Perhaps there is an analogy between the modern sense of powerlessness and Oates's conception of the artist at the mercy of character and situation. But Oates is also close in her vision to that of Henry James. James, echoing Turgenev (and Heraclitus), declared that character is "fate," a daimon that works its will. The artist does not synthesize; rather the personalities (the *disponibles*, the artist's available assets) somehow mysteriously "solicit" him to tell their stories and create their environments. For James art exerts its autonomy through character, testing the range of the artist's imagination.

For Oates art is created in a similar tension of wills: as fiction becomes an expression of "personality," it strains at its own formal limits. The artist is a collaborator and co-conspirator, imaginatively responding both to literary models and to human history, eventually submitting all work for revision—by future artists, by literary critics, and by the liberated energies of "autonomous" fictions. Ultimately the work turns on its creator: "the artist both creates and is created by his art."

Thus, Oates places the artist in the center of things, and not at a fabulator's remove. In place of solipsism she proposes a sacred marriage of art and society. In her criticism she attempts to project herself into the minds of other artists, revising and extending their conceptions. In her own imaginative writing she raises "influence" from hidden anxiety to an active principle, the yeast for her own peopling imagination; at the same time, she demonstrates a "negative capability," attempting to discover rather than impose character and situation. In the work of Joyce Carol Oates, then, many versions of "autonomy" come into play as she explores the multileveled relationships of self and world. Her fiction especially, preoccupied with the spasmodic, failed gestures of the ego, reflects a profound disenchantment with the old myth of personal autonomy; her novels and short stories seem preparations for a new, dynamic, daimonic synthesis.

Three short stories from Oates's collection, *Marriages and Infidelities*, are especially relevant to this discussion of her vision of the autonomy of self and art. Not to exert her authority as self-conscious shaper, but rather to emphasize her belief in the communal possibility of art, she selects and names three literary predecessors: "The Dead," "The Turn of the Screw," and "The Metamorphosis"; Joyce, James, and Kafka. Oates's own stories begin as examples of the genre of "influence," literary imitation; but the author also invites speculation about the nature of autonomy: the uniqueness of art, the influence of tradition, and the dangers and limitations of the old notions of selfhood played out in the modern scene. For Oates the original stories function as myths, familiar and available for retelling.

> These stories are meant to be autonomous stories, yet they are also testaments of my love and extreme devotion to these other writers; I imagine a kind of spiritual "marriage" between myself and them . . . let's say our "daimons" in the Yeatsian sense.

In her retelling, the "infidelities" as well as the "marriages" assume significance. Formal elements, style, narrative strategy and structure, patterns of imagery, are translated, recreated, distorted. Character relationships are cunningly inverted and both moral and aesthetic questions reopened. In the process the "heroic" dimensions of these fables are undercut and the self's fictions exposed.

By reimagining these stories (in Oates's own phrase) the author performs an interesting balancing act. She is at once something of a fabulator (manipulative, allusive) and more "modest," working in collaboration with her predecessors toward some new synthesis. These three stories provide a complex insight into Oates's mode of creation. She is versatile, eclectic. The figures Oates chooses for her literary testaments work out of quite different conceptions of the possibilities of autonomous action and even of the function of art; yet the author weds them all to her own vision.

Beyond his declaration that the artist was a self peculiarly vulnerable to the resonance of fact and character, James seems to envision the individual as an explorer in a formally-ordered society, a systematic structure of castes and stations. Focusing on personal relations within that system, and specifically within an elite clique, James exposes in probing and nuanced narrative the moral nature of human encounters. His central "consciousness" within each fictive structure rarely appeals to external dogma to govern or rationalize his or her choice: that would seem to minimize radically any moral action. Rather, his character exhibits a form of ethical autonomy, ultimately *seeing through* the various modes and shades of action, developing a "horrible sharp eye" for what is right in a world of competing value. The progress of moral vision determines the very shape of the fiction: "value" in a moral sense and "value" in a tonal, aesthetic sense become equivalent.

James explores the texture of individual moral decision, believing in its shaping power. Kafka despairs of man's ability to determine the course of his existence: for him, autonomy and even basic normative conceptions are myths, again in the dual sense that they suggest models of action while they falsify the nature of experience. "Justice" as a rational model governs the appeals of Kafka's *personae*; but their strategies are inevitably frustrated by the irreducible irrationality of the cosmos. Obviously Kafka's world lacks the social cohesiveness of the Jamesian milieu; yet a quasi-moral "order" functions in his fiction. Ironically its ineffectuality and irrelevance serve to emphasize the incongruity of human experience.

Both James and Kafka display characteristic narrative patterns that reflect their perception of ethical and artistic autonomy. For James the two somehow coincide: his stories are structured by successive layers of revelation; he peels away layers of mistaken perception, moving toward deeper levels of moral insight. In contrast, Kafka's fiction dramatizes the disjunction between dreams of autonomy and a baffling nightmare of impotence. As his characters continue to pursue just and moral resolutions, they are humbled and defeated.

James Joyce's narrative structure also offers a key to his vision of human value and the romance of personal autonomy. The linear patterns of James and Kafka conform to the deliberate (whether successful or failed) strategies of the questing self; Joyce's work insists upon its very shapelessness. His stories rise to fitful and momentary "epiphanies"—stimulated by encounters with reality but beyond the capacity of the characters to articulate; they subside, succumbing to some primordial rhythm, reaching a level at which human will and choice make little difference. For James and Kafka the chronological progression of narrative itself has significance, showing the causal relationship of choice and event: decision in James's case determines, and in Kafka's, mysteriously, does *not* determine, outcome. But in Joyce's work linear artistic shape is itself a mythic ideal, available as a fabulator's device, ironically contrasting with the shapelessness of the quotidian.

Given this brief and admittedly generalized summary, it is nevertheless clear that Oates has made some telling departures from both the moral and aesthetic positions of her three fictive predecessors as she reimagines the "germ" of their fiction. Her moral and social vision is less focused than that of James, less dependent on clarity of insight. The space between expectation and experience is not so gaping as in Kafka's world: the reality of Oates's observed world has somehow caught up with Kafka's nightmares. And Oates seems at once less affirmative and less submissive than Joyce. A closer examination of the three pairs of stories suggests various levels of marriages and infidelities.

James's "The Turn of the Screw" is a mystery story that defies solution, confounding all partial explanations by introducing a succession of unreliable witness-narrators who present the tale of two perverse ghosts and two corrupted innocents. The primary document, the diary of the overwrought governess, is problematic; and the central situation is mirrored in this distorted glass, leaving the reader to puzzle out the "truth" of the situation.

In a further turn of the screw James himself offers a crafty and ambiguous "authentication" of his sinister romance in the preface to the New York Edition. James describes himself as a "fabulist," coming upon a real but imperfectly glimpsed narrative which in turn serves as the germ of his own story. Having heard a "shadow of a shadow" of a haunting tale in a circle of acquaintances, James exploits it, aware of the tension between the artist's autonomy and his obligation to keep faith with external reality:

> To improvise with extreme freedom and yet at the same time without the possibility of ravage . . . that was here my definite business. The thing was to aim at absolute singleness, clearness

and roundness, and yet to depend on an imagination working freely, working (call it) with extravagance; by which law it wouldn't be thinkable except as free and wouldn't be amusing except as controlled.

James's "law" is curiously suggestive of Joyce Carol Oates's vision of the artist's method. Her own version of "The Turn of the Screw" is a "controlled" improvisation, an imaginative redaction of James's story as well as of the tangled threads of his biography. In the process Oates makes "extravagant" alterations in the tale and in the telling. James places his narrators at several removes from his "pair of abnormal agents," thus intensifying both the sense of mystery and the sense of evil. Oates takes an abnormal pair of guilt-ridden figures as twin centers of consciousness in her reimagined story; the horror of evil is minimized as she shifts her attention to its banality.

Parodying the Victorian journal, Oates simultaneously presents the diary entries of a sexually-starved young fop, sullenly attending his uncle in hopes of becoming his heir, and those of a neurasthenic elderly observer— James himself? The older man willfully misinterprets the young man's immoral behavior, transforming him into a figure more worthy of admiration; the youth, conscious of his own guilty secrets, misunderstands the elderly gentleman's behavior, believing him an accuser rather than an infatuated onlooker. Finally, the elderly man is driven to the youth's bedroom on some transparent errand; but even close to the actual scene, he cannot "see" the sordid truth. Rather, he expresses his passionate delusion in a cluster of letters to the mystified and terrified young fortune hunter.

Oates confronts both James's biography and Jamesian themes, mocking the term of "reality," the controlled extravagance, the inevitable distortions of the human eye. James's story becomes the occasion for Oates's own exploration of the strategies of the artist-voyeur, obsessed by dark appetites but eager to transform and sublimate them. The allusive presence of James in Oates's sketch itself suggests the ironic contrast between an ideal image of art and the pathetic, flawed gestures of ordinary existence. All attempts to rise above human appetites end in tragicomic confusion.

Kafka's "The Metamorphosis" is perhaps the quintessential modern story, a fable of transformation, suggesting ontological terror. The individual's willed resistance is futile, given the irresistible transforming energies which erupt out of the fabric of "normality." Commercial traveller Gregor Samsa awakens from uneasy dreams into a nightmare, transformed into a gigantic insect. Under his father's threatening eye and hand, unloved and finally loathed, Samsa at last submits to debasement and death, unable to articulate his human feelings and needs through his ugly carapace. Yet his family not only survives the experience but seems radically changed by it: Kafka ends his story with a sunlit image of the nubile sister, the smug, adoring parents. If Gregor's ego has been progressively defeated, the family's energies seem recharged.

Oates has confronted Kafka's story both as critic and artist. In her essay, "Kafka's Paradise," she suggests that Kafka fashions parables, not of despair and nihilism, but of "the ego's crisis as it approaches its own transcendence—the necessary anguish that precedes that 'radiance' mentioned so often in his work." Thus she interprets the ending of "The Metamorphosis" as the triumph of "life" over ego—"the conscious, private, grasping self":

> In the warm sunshine, new dreams arise, a totally new assessment of the family fortunes is made, and the girl, stretching her young body, is that final, wordless affirmation of life that Gregor . . . could not make: the "metamorphosis" is complete.

Oates's own imaginative revision traces a similar pattern: the transformation and dissolution of a personality, succeeded by a burst of warmth and light. But again, she makes significant shifts and revisions. Kafka had in a sense dramatized his own relationship with his father—the relationship of a despised "insect" and a loveless tyrant—in Gregor's story. Oates transfers the identity of victim from son to father, perhaps more suitable to a society in which the young are worshiped and emulated. Not only is her central figure, the father-victim, less pitiable and less sympathetic, but the child emerges whole, apparently untouched, and in the role of unconscious artist seems to recreate the story from fragments of memory.

Gregor is a stock figure, a commercial traveller; Oates tells the story of a modern bourgeois stereotype, an automobile salesman, who is suddenly rendered inarticulate, incontinent, and physically grotesque by a shattering nervous breakdown. His collapse also comes without warning, but out of his own psychological lower depths, out of an alien dream, exploding along the leading edge of a cracked surface. Yet, inured to his routine, devoted to the clichés of the American middle class, he cannot even recognize the terror as his own:

> There had been a body, a kind of mummy, lying very still beneath heavy covers. Sheets pulled up to the chin. A faceless face. Formless bulges, ridges. A mystery. The figure had appeared in

> his mind's eye and had held itself there for some minutes, fright-
> ening him. . . . But it was not his dream. It must have belonged
> to someone else. . . . Someone was infecting him with bad dreams.

Unlike Gregor he cannot even submit to his fate; his detachment from reality negates the possibility of suicidal resignation. His dilemma may be irreversible, but it is not inexplicable. The father makes a straitjacketed exit; his child rushes out to the surviving mother, into the garden, the sunlight, the open air.

Kafka's shadow falls across Oates's story, pointing up its parodic elements and its satire of the diminished contemporary scene. The threat of the punishing father that haunted Kafka's vision suggested an overarching if malignant promise of egocentric potency. In punishing the father Oates neutralizes the spectre of authority; in naming the evil and rendering the metamorphosis apprehensible, she dissolves the mystery. She explodes the myth of "autonomous man" and at the same time drains the story of metaphysical significance. The fumbling modern self of Oates's "The Metamorphosis" witnesses realistic, ordinary, demonstrable horrors; somehow he regroups his own forces and moves toward the light, baffled rather than reanimated by the "radiance." Yet Oates does offer some hope: the tale remains to be retold, and the teller has survived long past the time of anguish.

Perhaps Oates's most elaborate "re-imagining" is her version of "The Dead." In his original story in *The Dubliners,* Joyce explored the intrusive and chill presence of the "dead"—dead hopes, dead promises, dead loves and lovers—which surface inexplicably in the rites of the living. Joyce ends his story with a lyrical submission to what Richard Ellman calls "mutuality"—the recognition that "all men feel and lose feeling, all interact, all warrant . . . sympathy." As the snow falls on Joyce's central characters, the "swooning" narrator Gabriel Conroy and his wife, lost in dreams of a long-lost lover, it falls universally, on living and dead alike, covering inanimate landmarks and human monuments. In this sense the "snow" obliterates all human acts and choices; even the shape of the tale itself is submerged in its falling rhythm.

Oates again shifts the story's central consciousness in her reimagined "The Dead": she focuses not on the bemused and disappointed man but on the woman who eludes his embrace, who feels she has lost the best possibilities of life and love. In Joyce's story the woman has been loved by a tubercular troubador, who had romantically risked death to serenade her—clearly, a scene taken from the stock repertoire of autonomous heroic gestures. In Oates's tale the woman is a writer and sometime college professor, addicted, ravaged, and lonely; once loved by a young campus radical whose life was brutally foreshortened by drugs and the violence of student demonstrations. Joyce's touchstones of value, the traditions and native art of Ireland, are also reduced in the translation: they seem fitfully paralleled by the crumbling requirements and standards of American academic life. The heroine's academic integrity is in almost ludicrous contrast to the compromises and accommodations of her second-rate Catholic university. The warmth and hospitality of a Dublin evening is ironically reimagined as the empty courtesies and envious slanders of a college literary reception.

The heroine seems to defy her former colleagues in an autonomous gesture by leaving the university and turning to art; but, Oates reveals, she is more immediately motivated by a need to escape the tangle of her personal life. She is destructive to herself and others; she nearly causes the destruction of another marriage after destroying her own. Yet marriage itself has a special value in this story:

> Marriage was the deepest, most mysterious, most profound exploration open to man: because she had failed did not change that belief. This plunging into another's soul, this pressure of bodies together, so brutally intimate, was the closest one could come to a sacred adventure.

Affirming marriage as a sacrament, Oates offers her own contemporary vision of the mystical possibilities of human intercourse.

Curiously her heroine is plunging into another sort of "marriage." Like Oates herself she is engaged in a project of "re-imagining" the work of her literary predecessors. Yet like the fabulators whom Oates criticizes she cannot see art's communal possibilities; this seems art's final spasm:

> "I don't exist as an individual but only as a completion of a tradition, the end of something, not the best part of it but only the end," she explained, wondering if she was telling the truth or if this was all nonsense.

Depleted, Oates's heroine writes literature of exhaustion; narcotics, alcohol, random sexuality are her palliatives, undermining both art and life. At the end of the story she too lies "swooning," unable to give or receive love. In Oates's version of "The Dead" the "snow" falling at the end is not a sign of community or mutuality. Ironically it suggests the pathetic and suicidal isolation in the "snow" of drugs (cocaine); an escape from the harrowing demands of profane life, rather than a submission to its sacred rhythm.

Many common threads run through these allusive fictions. Most obvious are Oates's fabulistic reversals and substitutions. She reimagines the victimizer as victim, reverses the roles of son and father, man and woman, plays out ironic variations of love. In a sense Oates's "homage" to her predecessors speaks in moral tones of the trivialization of contemporary life, a downward spiral since the "Modernist" revolution of consciousness. But the stories do more than exploit surface ironies for social and political comment. They are a dramatic critique of the myth of personal autonomy. In this world of shifting forms and identities, with the diminution of the sense of individual potency, the focus of fiction shifts from the defiant to the defeated self. These three stories dramatize what Oates herself has stated in her essays: the cult of individual personality and "ego" is no longer meaningful.

There is also a progressive devaluation of the creator-hero in Oates's reimagining, a demythicization of the artist's proud autonomy as aesthetic strategies are revealed and parodied. The Jamesian artist-observer is transformed and revealed as a voyeur; artistic predilections are connected with prurient interests. Perceptions are so off-the-mark that the growth of the self is stunted. In this post-Freudian age mysteries are translated into the language of psychoanalysis: the creation of literature is imagined as a sublimation of drives; demonic metamorphosis is reduced to a failure of nerves; mystic immolation is a state simulated by pills and self-delusion; selfless romantic gestures are exposed as self-aggrandizing pantomimes or irresponsible acts of violence. Thus, seen in both the moral and aesthetic shadow of their masterful predecessors, these allusive stories might be taken as fables of entropy.

Oates takes great risks in her assertion of the "impermanence" of the artifact and the "delusion" of egocentrism. In attacking the old myths of autonomy, in suggesting that the artist's angle of vision is susceptible of infinite refraction and diffusion, and that selfhood is a corrupting metaphor, she opens the way to chaos and disintegration. The artist's own alternatives seem radically delimited: the conception of art as an object of value falters in the peeling away of old visions of self and world.

The first story in the same collection offers a curious and even comic glimpse of Oates's own projected alternative: a vision of communal art in the aftermath of the death of individual ego. Oates introduces *Marriages and Infidelities* with a story called "The Sacred Marriage." Although she does not explicitly allude to it in the title, the story is highly suggestive of another tale by Henry James, "The Aspern Papers."

James's story of a "publishing scoundrel," significantly enough, explores the moral and aesthetic problem of art's influence on human behavior. It charts the actions of a literary parasite, so obsessed with his professional ambitions that he will do anything to obtain the unpublished manuscripts of a dead poet: falsification of identity, breach of promise, invasion of privacy (even the privacy of the death chamber), betrayal of love and gentle hopes. Prodded by his publish-or-perish appetite, he exhibits a moral blindness so absolute that he is incapable of *knowing* anything: he can never even know with certainty if the papers themselves truly exist. In James's moral sphere such a failure of perception is the unpardonable sin.

In Oates's story there are no such ambiguities to sift through. There *are* manuscripts, boxes and stacks of them, and they are freely and willingly presented to Howard, the dazed and disbelieving scholar. Even the dead poet's wife comes under his stewardship, freely and unconditionally, or so it seems. The effect of this artistic and scholarly "find" is startling. Howard becomes possessed by the personality of the dead poet as he assumes responsibility for manuscripts and wife, and he feels his own previously "aimless life" all at once taking shape.

Newly born as the dead poet's surrogate, feeling autonomous, Howard falls in love with the widow and begins to edit and winnow the pile of unpublished material: he is recreated by his communal bond with his predecessor. Thus he is stunned when the widow admits another scholar into the sanctum sanctorum and initiates a now familiar ritual, offering freely both the papers and herself. Outraged at the amorality of the gesture and the personal betrayal, Howard suddenly finds his own pursuit of art detestable. "A living woman," he rages, "was worth more than a dead man's novel, any dead man's novel or his poetry or any poetry. That was a fact."

Yet such "fact" does not provide Howard with avenues of action; indeed, he had been virtually impotent in a world governed by similar realities. Sensing the return of his former "aimlessness" as his new identity begins to crumble, he gropes through the dead man's papers, blindly seeking assistance. He comes upon an unpublished "parable" that has previously escaped his attention but which uncannily prefigures his own situation: it describes the last days of a poetic genius, his calculated marriage, his death, and his resurrection, achieved through his wife's curatorship and her body, and a succession of faithful and imaginative collaborators.

Shocked by this "fiction" as he had never been moved by life's random pressures, Howard feels the loss of ontological security; has he been dissolved into a fictive creation? Has he become a puppet serving a dead man's will? He flees the house, the papers, and the widow. But without them he now lacks even the resources for physical survival. His car careens wildly, out of control on mountain descents. "Why should he continue living?" he wonders. "He felt his face, his body, his very identity seeping back inside him, inside the amorphous shapelessness of his past. He was becoming an ordinary man again."

Both James's story and Oates's tale explore the relationship of life and art, the sifting of moral and aesthetic imperatives, the possibilities of reconciling the "ordinary" and the "artistic" choice. In "The Aspern Papers" the essential venality of the hero protects him from engulfment, but at the cost of both human and artistic fulfillment. Paradoxically, Howard's lack of selfishness, his ill-defined personal identity, make him vulnerable to the insatiable appetites of a dead—but autonomous—artist. "If Howard Dean had been lied to, betrayed, what did that matter?" he asks himself. "The important thing was that he had seen the Pearce papers." Fighting off his deathward spiral, buoyed by the resurgent, vicarious energies of his predecessor, he dedicates himself to the "sacred marriage." Howard Dean finally asserts his autonomy, only to give up his ordinary "joke of a life"; he overcomes the anxiety of literary influence only by losing himself in a prefabricated design. Surrendering the remnants of ego and even his sense of moral propriety, he survives to serve his fabulator, Pearce. Oates—giving the screw a final turn—mocks them both: "The Sacred Marriage" becomes a parable of the dangerous and seductive autonomy of art.

In her essays Joyce Carol Oates speaks confidently of the welcome death of the ego and criticizes the fabulator's self-promoting display. But in her fiction she dramatizes the ambiguous attractions of fabulation; her own skillful pieces demonstrate its power even as they attempt to expose its corruption. Her stories show the difficulty of survival without the sustaining myth of "autonomous man" in a world both threatening and irrational. The inherited structuring of things, glimpsed in an array of literary allusions, only seems to underscore the diminished moral and aesthetic possibilities of contemporary society and contemporary art. Does Oates feel some sympathy as well as scorn for the fabulator who, finding the world debased, establishes his own ego at its center and substitutes aesthetic "plots" for paranoia? More importantly, how do her characters, after dropping the ego's last defenses, come to resist the terror of formlessness and the alternative threat of extrinsic manipulation? What lies beyond the prison of the self?

In her explicit literary "marriages" Oates is chiefly concerned with the failure of old dreams of the potent self to deal with a world of ontological nightmare. In a positive sense, by reworking and reimagining forms and themes and stories, she demonstrates in contrast the inexhaustible energies and resources of the artistic tradition and imagination. Yet despite her professed dislike for the adolescent, anachronistic "I" and the solipsistic poet, the old myths continue to exert their shaping power on her fiction, a power that must be both demonstrated and resisted. In her more "autonomous" and less-allusive stories, and especially in her novels, Oates tests the limits of James's law and the possibilities of Joyce's mutualism. Like Kafka, conditioned by the self's hungry demands but longing for radiance, Joyce Carol Oates offers momentary glimpses of a "new heaven, new earth," transcending the struggles of the individual ego and the self-serving defiance of the autonomous artist.

MARY ALLEN

The Terrified Women
of Joyce Carol Oates

The overwhelming fact in the lives of Joyce Carol Oates's best characters is economic: "The greatest realities are physical and economic; all the subtleties of life come afterward. Intellectuals have forgotten, or else they never understood, how difficult it is to make one's way up from a low economic level, to assert one's will in a great crude way. It's so difficult. You have to go through it. You have to be poor." Oates's sympathies are so obviously with these poor that her treatment of women characters is frequently divided more clearly along the lines of poverty and affluence than as some writers make a division, between the types of the bitch mother and the dull wife. The women of the middle and upper classes, particularly as they are satirized, seldom come to life as her lower-class women do. Among the latter are those who somewhat obtusely survive better than anyone else, such as Loretta Botsford of *them,* and the more passive and intelligent sufferers like her daughter Maureen Wendall, Oates's most excellent creation and one of the most interesting women in the literature of the sixties.

In their efforts at economic survival, Oates's male characters traditionally pursue more varied methods, both legitimate and illegitimate, than her women do. Men enter the life of the streets and are in closer touch with the world's goods, even if they are not to possess them. Women, in their more limited spheres, are resigned to improving their financial status rather by attachment to men. Clara Walpole (*A Garden of Earthly Delights*) raises

---

From *The Necessary Blankness.* © 1976 by the Board of Trustees of the University of Illinois. University of Illinois Press, 1976.

herself to a life on her own farm through her manipulation of the wealthy Revere. The toughness of women like Clara is not found, perhaps because it is not demanded, in, for instance, Updike's young women, who are adequately provided for. His middle-class wives are not forced to claw their way to financial security. The sense of power (which usually breaks down) in Oates's lower-class women, developed as the men disappear or destroy themselves through some form of violence, is both frightening and refreshing after the many accounts of sterile middle-class women whose leisure allows them to become bored neurotics.

Clara Walpole is bitterly determined to escape the doom of her mother's life—a woman first shown to us as she is trapped in her third pregnancy, traveling as a migrant worker. The facts of Mrs. Walpole's life flow together in a blur. She never understands or controls. "The women had no opinion; opinions belonged to men." Clara flees such a situation to offer herself shamelessly to Lowry, the most immediately available man of any appeal; she literally walks into his room and turns her life over to him. Such a response has nothing to do with love, of course, but is the way a man and a woman painfully, irrevocably collide and become bound by sexual and other destructive forces. Clara gladly leaves her father, but she soon wishes he would find her and kill Lowry. (And such a fantasy in one of these stories is not to be taken lightly.) She eventually escapes Lowry, but only for a time, as she sets herself up with Revere's wealth.

Clara, afraid at first of being crushed like her mother, when she has her own child and property, is terrified of losing them. Underlying the calm that prevails as she works in her garden is the dread of Lowry's return, which is in some way a threat to everything established in her new life. Harboring her hatred of him, Clara carefully cultivates their delicate son Swan, a sensitive, nervous child. Since violence is bound to be the outcome of inward tensions, considering that few things remain abstract for Oates, we await an explosion in Swan's future.

Clara's garden is not the Eden it appears to be but the literal sign of economic gain, just as Revere represents concrete wealth and power, not romantic attachment. The idea of marrying for money is a pragmatic law of life neither Clara nor Oates would call into question. Clara's icy materialism and her eventual insanity are not the result of a wrong choice regarding Revere but merely deterministic responses to negative conditions. If her very secularized garden is to remind us that Eden is no more, it is a version of the author's own expiation of the supernatural which she says was worked out of her system in her first novel, *With Shuddering Fall*. Even when people do obey "God's commands," she states, they are not rewarded. Living in this world is "a sufficiently intricate hopeless problem itself without bringing in another world, bringing in an extra dimension."

When Lowry demonically appears to break the surface peace of Clara's pastoral life, her panic is handled with the great skill the author has developed for such scenes. Against her will Clara is once again drawn to her lover, who shatters the careful surface of the life she has so painstakingly built:

> She stared miserably at the floor. Everything was draining out of her, all her strength, all the hatred that had kept Lowry close to her for so long. It struck her that she had fed on this hatred and that it had kept her going, given her life. Now that he was here and standing before her, she could not remember why she had hated him.
>
> "You bastard," she whispered. "Coming back here like this— You—"
>
> "Let me make you quiet," Lowry said.
>
> She looked up at his smile, which was exactly like the smile she remembered.

Determined that Swan shall have more control over his life than she has had, Clara tries to keep him from a knowledge of Lowry; when he comes, the boy is shunted out of the way, but he feels the degree of his mother's anxiety. Beneath her attempt to control is the greater sense of things crumbling. Even the land they own offers no security. Clara's tenuous hold on her realities is reflected in her son, whose tension erupts first in an accidental shooting of his stepbrother, and finally in the shooting of his stepfather and himself. Clara is last seen in a nursing home dwindling in a passive state of insanity, the feminine alternative to the explosive response of Swan.

Under the surface of the toughest of Oates's people, like those of Barth, Pynchon, Purdy, and others, is a desperate emptiness. Both men and women face a void; but men are typically much more active in attempting to fill that void than are women, who are more likely simply to collide with men's violence in their sexual encounters. While sexual activity provides the raucous action of the fabulators, and for a writer like Updike remains the best and often the only communication between men and women, for Oates it is more a hard fact of existence, like others which women must frequently deal with sheerly as matters of economic expediency. A woman will inevitably be used by men. Whether or not she can profit financially from the experience is the crucial matter. It is true that serious female writers seldom write explicitly of sex, but it is not mere reticence that is responsible for the swift,

non-erotic scenes of lovemaking for Oates. Women most often offer themselves to men as business transactions, and the sooner the matter is done
with the better. The sexual act is not necessarily repulsive, but frequently
women feel nothing, simply allowing their bodies to be used for pay. In this
Oates understands prostitution as do none of her contemporaries for its
basically economic aspects. Her coldly pragmatic view of it makes Updike's
treatment of Ruth, for example, seem absurdly romantic.

For some women, more often those of the middle class, sexual experience is painful. In a fascinating story, "Unmailed, Unwritten Letters," a
woman's thoughts to her parents, her husband, her lover, and her lover's
daughter, who sends bitter notices in the mail, she claims that the second
time a woman falls in love "the sensation is terrifying, bitter, violent." At
the age of thirty she would say good-by to love and to the act of love. "A
woman in the act of love feels no joy but only terror, a parody of labor,
giving birth. Torture. Heartbeat racing at 160, 180 beats a minute, where is
joy in this, what is this deception, this joke. Isn't the body itself a joke?"

Some women are necessarily conscious of their bodies as their only
equipment in an ultimately concrete world, and they pay careful but grudg-
ing attention to the care of skin, hair, and figure, as they must to attract
men. But since beauty often brings on the abuse of men, women frequently
make themselves hideously fat, or ugly with misshapen clothes. The body is
a liability, after all, always out of control, the center of pain and the source
of excretions that proliferate in Oates's work: vomit, blood, diseased tissue,
menstrual blood, and the newborn child itself, the most terrible excretion of
all.

There are a great many fat people in Oates's fiction, fat often as a result
of efforts to fill up the empty self. (Since the author's sympathies are primarily with the poor, she makes abundance particularly gross.) Richard
Everett, the boy murderer of his mother in *Expensive People,* at the telling
of his story is a 250-pound eighteen-year-old, planning suicide by eating
until his stomach bursts. Parents endlessly stuff their children with treats.
The second section of *Wonderland* is an orgy of eating, with the monstrous
Dr. Pedersen guiding his family into one gargantuan meal after another as
they grow into helpless giants. Fat girls balloon perversely fatter, often
merely to spite men. Dr. Pedersen's daughter Hilda arrives at dinner in
burlap to rankle her expensively dressed father. The scene where he coerces
her into a dress shop and hovers in the lobby to pass judgment on the clothes
she models is unforgettable. How splendidly Oates understands such things
as the misery of tugging on a tight dress in one of those stuffy chambers of
a clothing store, pestered by a clerk who is bound to enter at any moment

to pull at the zipper and remark that the ill-fitting garment looks fine. Hilda is sure that the dress she must tug on will rip. Her father sees her in it and bellows out "No!" to his blimp-like daughter, who trots back to try again.

The male characters of the family are as fat as the females but never so disgusting, and never does their ugliness represent such a vilification of self. Dr. Pedersen's unfortunate and very fat wife is found prostrate in her bathroom by the innocent Jesse, their adopted son (the protagonist of the novel), who is also an enormous blob of fat. She convinces Jesse to help her escape her monster husband, and the two of them perform a fantastic scene of eating in a neighboring town—one giant meal after another. (He consumes an entire Chinese dinner with his hands while waiting outside her hotel room.) Mrs. Pedersen refuses to answer the calls of her husband, but she is quite incapable of creating a life apart from him. Perhaps the most pathetic fat person of all, she is given a gruesome sympathy reserved for physically grotesque women, which surpasses any pity we might feel for the desperate Jesse, distraught as he is with his more profound problems. He goes on to a thinner more varied life, if not a satisfying one, while the Pedersen women remain trapped in their fat.

Both beautiful and unbeautiful women masochistically attempt to make themselves repulsive to men. Since so much distress comes with sexual involvement, it is preferable to discourage men by being ugly. In a story entitled "Normal Love" a woman of forty desires but fears the attentions of her husband of many years. "Why am I not at peace, being forty years old?" she asks herself; "a woman wants to rake her body with her nails, streaming blood, she wants to gash her face so that no man need look at it." She wants to be safe, and to be safe a woman must be beyond sex. Her sex draws her back into life, and with that comes a frightening loss of control, which is the case for the beautiful widow in "What Is the Connection between Men and Women?" After her husband dies her life is as blank as the white china in the shop where she works, but she feels that no calamity can touch her. Then another man comes along and draws her from deathlike boredom to that only other alternative for a woman, a threatening connection with a man. Some women obliterate their beauty but at the same time plunge self-destructively into such a connection. In "Pastoral Blood" a very pretty young girl named Grace, a week before she is to be married, suddenly proceeds to make love to strangers. Repulsed by the kind of femininity she has represented, she ritualistically replaces her pink flowered dress with a black blouse and a black striped skirt, attire representative of a lower-class promiscuity. Thwarting "the work of centuries, civilizations, to bring forth such a product. . . . Pretty girl!," she drives out of town to her new fate.

The most original and stunning account of a woman's masochistic delight in making herself gross to men is the unforgettable "At the Seminary." An obviously neurotic family of three—father, mother, and fat, fat daughter—visit the son at the seminary. Sally resents the emphasis placed on her brother's pious life, with its denial of the physical, and the seriousness with which his minor problems are discussed. Her problems are the crucial ones. She hates smug mothers, disapproves of children, in short is disgusted by life. "Her mother had wanted her to be pretty, she thought, and deliberately she was not pretty." She revels in her obesity and is charmed at the seminary to detect the start of her menstrual period. Before the shocked but gracious priest, and her family, she crosses the room slamming her feet loudly to the floor, giggling all the while as the menstrual blood dribbles horribly down her legs and into her shoes before the gaze of the incredulous men. She triumphs with the excuse, "I never asked God to make me a woman!"

Women's mortifying effects to their bodies, committed in spite against the importance placed upon appearance or as a direct design against their specific antagonists, are also a way of reacting to the genuine fear of assault. A combination of these motives in a particularly paranoid form appears in "Stalking," in which a heavy-set girl of thirteen fantasizes that she is being followed by an "Adversary." Gretchen, who like other fat girls flaunts her ugliness in defiance of the commercialized standard of beauty, also uses it as a defense against her imagined pursuer. There are hints that she could be a handsome girl, but out of disgust and fear she makes herself dowdy and sexless. As an attack upon methods of beautification, she smears lipstick (which she has stolen from a drugstore) on the mirror in the ladies' room of a department store, shoves a towel in the toilet, and flushes. But rather than try to actually destroy her adversary, she fantasizes his death by envisioning pools of blood in his front hallway.

Women's fear of violent action is usually accompanied by a fascination with it. If given the choice between duplicating their mothers' trapped lives at home or joining men in their wild destruction, most make the second choice. Such is the story of Mae in "What Death with Love Should Have to Do," a paradigm of the novel *With Shuddering Fall*. The image of a woman clinging to a man's back as he roars along on his motorcycle is an appropriate picture of her parasitic and dangerous relationship to him. Male power is enhanced by man's use of the machine, and a woman cleaves to these mysterious forces. But as Jules Wendall of *them* points out, women know nothing about machines. And this deficiency increases their sense of powerlessness in a power-driven world. Mae's wild ride on the motorcycle brings about a miscarriage, and as the bleeding begins (Oates's penchant for blood) she pleads for her lover to stop. Riding along in the wind he cannot hear her. When they finally do stop, she vomits (another familiar Oates touch). Despite these destructive effects, Mae chooses the male world of energy and action, seeing herself only as the "anonymous hard-faced girl surrounded by men." She dies from the miscarriage.

Mae's counterpart in *With Shuddering Fall,* Karen Herz, also wills her life from a drab existence to a dangerous one, with similar results. Karen is drawn to her father's brute power and is similarly attracted to Shar and his race cars. Like many of Oates's women, she at first mistakenly imagines that men in all their activity have a control over their lives that she does not have. But Shar is badly out of control with his cars, causing collisions both on and off the racetrack. Oates (who learned about cars from *Hot Rod Magazine*) makes excellent use here of the destructive potential of man's favorite machine, both as a literal element in her naturalistic detail and as an image to illustrate sexual and emotional collisions.

Karen enters Shar's life as she once intentionally dashed in front of a speeding car and was almost killed. The destructive and the sexual are perfectly united, the lovers even referring to each other as killers. Despairing her lack of control over love and its devastation, Karen twists her face into ugly patterns before the mirror to fend off her lover and love. But she suffers the usual pregnancy, which results in a miscarriage that almost kills her, and her dealings with Shar bring on the expected insanity. Back at her own home she is presumably at peace, but such a possibility seems unlikely. Both Karen and Shar suffer the effects of violence, but with a difference: Shar at least has more to do with how his life will end. As Karen says, " 'His death was no accident: only his life is.' " Her only choice is for the violent over the sedentary. After that decision, she is a victim.

Despite the frequency of violence in the writing of Joyce Carol Oates, and she often treats it brilliantly, its truth borne out to us by newspaper accounts every day, she is even better at showing the quiet terror that so often lies under the surface of normal things, *the apprehension of violence.* On an ordinary afternoon a suburban housewife drives into a parking lot of a major department store and imagines a man there to be following her: "My heart begins to pound absurdly, I know there is no danger and yet my muscles stiffen as if in expectation of danger, the very shape of my skeleton tensing as if to receive a blow. . . . The elevator comes. The door opens. I step inside, the man steps quickly inside, for a moment I feel a sense of panic, as if inside me a door is opening suddenly upon nothing, upon blackness." Nothing happens. But the chill evoked in this everyday setting is astonishing. Many of Oates's best scenes, like this one, reveal women's solitary, haunting fears, especially of men. In this the author is at least as effective with her more affluent women as she is with her poor ones.

"Where Are You Going, Where Have You Been?" is probably the most powerful example of fear in a normal setting. Connie, a fifteen-year-old, is ever so typical a teenager of the fifties—arguing with her mother about not wanting to clean her room, using junky hair spray, considering her older, unmarried sister a social disaster. To her friends she complains about her mother, but her irritations are not unusual for a teenage girl. Such are the normalcies of a life drawn without a flaw and with just the right touches of sleaziness. One dull Sunday afternoon, with her parents off to a barbecue at an aunt's house, Connie spends the day drying her hair in the sun and daydreaming of love. A gold-tinted jalopy pulls up in the drive and out comes Arnold Friend, who wants her to go for a ride. A thousand Sunday afternoons in a thousand small towns are like this one. After a long, half-bored, half-flirtatious conversation, a girl finally gives in and goes for the ride, which usually results in more suggestion than action.

In her boredom Connie is mildly curious as to the stranger she has seen only once before, but she dawdles about going for a ride with him. She has things to do. Things. He laughs, and they jostle for position casually for a good length of the story until something frightening begins to happen, slowly, quietly, with very little surface indication. Mr. Friend lets Connie know that he wants more than a Sunday drive and will not stop until he gets it. The subtle strain of paranoia most women feel about the possibilities of sexual attack turns chillingly into a real threat for Connie. Her flippant, easy approach freezes in her as she dares to realize the threat, which Friend refers to in such a proper way: " 'It's real nice and you couldn't ask for nobody better than me, or more polite. I always keep my word. I'll tell you how it is, I'm always nice at first, the first time.' " Under the impact of fear the familiar kitchen is no longer familiar to Connie, and the screen door that a moment ago was such a homey, teasing barrier for her becomes a startlingly flimsy protection from what Mr. Friend now represents. His promise not to come in the house after her is more disturbing than a blunt demand might be, for we know he will enter when he is ready. The screen door is slight, he observes; locking it will never keep him out if he cares to come in. Friend's language is commonplace, filled with words Connie's mother might have said a few hours before—" 'Now, you be a good girl' "—more frightening than any obscenity could be. Eventually, with the stiffness terror puts into this once-cocky girl, Connie watches herself push open the screen door and go out to Arnold Friend, into a sunlit afternoon and a landscape she can no longer recognize. The story exhibits no violence. But it is more terrifying than those that do, with a fear that transforms familiar objects and the landscape in a way that suggests that they will never be quite normal again. A short passage of time is immense. Such treatment of the anticipation of violence is Oates's great strength, not the account of actual violence, which is often anticlimactic.

Women's fear of men is seldom dramatized through scenes of rape and mutilation. When such acts occur the information comes by way of the news or through gossip. The distance of these events in comparison with other acts of violence—there are several closeups of murder—is in keeping with the emphasis on the *fear* perpetrated by the thought of rape and its accompanying brutality, rather than on the acts themselves. What woman has not at some time imagined rape, especially when the news announces that it has been committed a block from her home? After reading of a rape-murder in her neighborhood, a woman cannot pass a familiar doorway without being afraid. Most women never will be attacked, but there is no way they can insure their safety against a threat that is not limited to any particular social or economic class, age group, or location. Oates never allows us to forget the sheer amount of violence in America. If we never encounter it directly ourselves, we will probably know someone who does. The fact that some form of brutality occurs on our streets every few minutes is the kind of knowledge that rules the minds of Oates's people.

The affluent housewife who is freed of the economic burdens and other pressures of poverty is even more likely to be obsessed by quiet terrors than is her poorer counterpart. Oates's later stories frequently turn to the fears of the suburban woman, and in dealing with this subject she is much more effective than she is in satirizing suburbia's emptiness, also coming closer to her own experience in the treatment of anxiety than in scenes of brutality. *The Wheel of Love* volume of stories, which does not contain as much violence as the earlier collections (although the most recent novels deal with her usual dosage of blood), is particularly effective. In one of the rare interviews with Oates, a clue to her own fearful perceptions is very revealing. She is sitting in her back yard, which leads to a lake; the water is calm, the day is mild, and "far out on the sunny river a small blue boat is rocking gently with two boys in it. She says softly, 'I don't like to see them out there. These boats turn over very easily and you can't get them upright again. If that happened, I'm not sure what I could do.' " This is exactly the sense of disturbance that she portrays so powerfully in her quiet women of refinement, who feel incapable of dealing with dangerous action or even strong emotions.

One such account is "What Is the Connection between Men and Women?," in which a man simply glances at a woman in a supermarket and the terror of lust is upon her. Back in her comfortable apartment she sits alone and tense, jarred by the ringing of the phone. She waits. When the man comes to her door at five o'clock in the morning, after they have both been awake all night, she answers his knock, slides back the bolt, and "everything comes open, comes apart." A man's arrival is characteristically treated as a fearful but inevitable happening, bringing the disintegration that leads to life and to madness. This effect is found in "6:27" in dealing with the return of a woman's ex-husband. She is a hairdresser, nervously edging through her day in anticipation of the fearful moment he will enter the shop. He calls her and then hangs up, but never appears in the story, which ends at 6:25 with Glenda and her unwanted son in the supermarket. We never know what happens at 6:27.

Just as effectively as Oates shows the fear of the strange or the estranged man, she captures the anxieties of a woman regarding the familiar and apparently trusted man. In "Normal Love" Mrs. York respects and "loves" her husband, who is never cruel but who does preserve a disturbing silence. The trappings of normal life in a contemporary American suburb give what should be a comfortable surface—the neighborhood supermarket with its tinseled tree for Christmas, the family meals prepared with care, and the sound of the telephone. But alone in her quiet home Mrs. York cannot place herself and jumps nervously whenever the phone rings. She misses her children, who are at school, but the thought of their return is threatening. "Do they want to damage me, my flesh? No. Does my husband want to damage me? No." And at the hairdresser's the chatter drifts casually to the topic of thalidomide babies. The regular schedule Mrs. York and her family keep shows no deviations that would be disturbing. Her husband, a doctor, has a drink every night at five, and they eat dinner punctually at six. Although she considers herself a blessed woman, loving the very knives and forks that feed her family, alternating with her pleasure in these signs of "normal" love she envisions herself retching over the bathroom sink.

It is common enough to show the calm distances in the modern marriage, often its sheer vacancy. But in the specific quality of fear felt in these vacancies Oates gives us something peculiarly her own. It is the predominant feeling her married women have. Unlike most of Oates's contemporaries, she has little to say of sex in marriage, making its conspicuous by its absence. Perhaps her women repress thoughts of sex. Either they fear sexual experience or their emotions are not deeply touched by it any more than the act of prostitution affects women who are forced into it for their livelihood.

Women seem to make love in their sleep. Mrs. York remembers being pregnant but not how she came to her condition. But far from being at peace, she is disturbed when her husband even looks at her.

The texture of this normal life is interrupted when Dr. York finds a girl's purse in the vacant lot by their home. The owner is later discovered as only a torso floating in the river. The fact of the girl's murder is related to Mrs. York by a friend at a party; the victim was apparently murdered by the lover she had spent the previous night with in a motel. Such an event is naturally a piece of gossip, and it is necessarily related to Mrs. York because her husband discovered the girl's purse. But there is a foreboding connection between Mrs. York's feelings of dread and the brutalizing of the girl, which is nothing so specific as anxiety for her life, since it is her kindly husband she fears. And he would never harm her. Would he? Mrs. York's awareness of what a woman's physical appeal can lead to—the girl's murder—is related to her desire to gash her face, as an escape. She is too refined and controlled, however, to do anything like this. Oates's later stories increasingly deal with the tensions of people who are locked in without the release of violence, with an emphasis on the strangeness and anxiety in their seemingly amiable relationships. The bizarre murder in "Normal Love" is kept at a distance (although not too far distant) and is used not as a direct threat to the suburban woman but as a focal point for her anxiety.

The story "Puzzle" poses the question of what brings people together in marriage, and then what holds them together, the queerest puzzle of all. The connection between men and women in these stories is especially disturbing, for there is no suggestion of a happiness to mitigate the fear involved in the bond. There are no lighthearted, joyful, or even sensuous experiences. But a dangerous association is preferred to the alternative of separation, which results in lifelessness for the woman.

There is no actual violence in "Puzzle," only the memory of the death of the couple's child that occurred years before, which is made crucial to their present relationship. The young boy was drowned in a drainage ditch. His mother, who has no other children, is understandably awkward and upset whenever she meets children on the street. The memory of the lost child provokes hostility between the couple, but at the same time it connects them. Like the murdered girl in "Normal Love," the death of the boy serves as a focal point for the inherent tension of the marriage. Meanwhile, the woman is afraid of her husband and at times wishes he were dead. One evening as they arrive home late she plans to announce that she is leaving him. Oates is expert at making real the dread of these people as they enter their own seemingly safe home. The husband goes to the refrigerator, his wife waits nervously, and then he surprises her by saying it was his own carelessness that was responsible for the accident that took their boy's life. This sudden vulnerability is apparently the clue to the puzzle that keeps this couple together. She is now unable to leave him. They embrace, and she admits (as so many of Oates's characters feel) that she understands nothing outside of the present moment.

The children that inevitably result from even the briefest encounters with men are as unfortunate as the connections that bring them about. The mother, or ex-mother as she calls herself in "Puzzle," who laments the loss of her child, would probably be pained by his existence if he were alive. Childbirth is another of the violent disasters that make women bitter and afraid; it is bloody and painful, very often fatal. Women seldom commit the murders that fill Oates's fiction, but when they do become violent they are most likely to vent themselves against their children, perhaps because only in this connection are they physically superior to their antagonists.

One of the few times a woman commits murder is in an early story, "Swamps." An animal-like, pregnant girl wandering in the swamps, scorned by the townspeople, is finally taken in by an old man who cares for her. After giving birth to her child she drowns it, leaving it head down in a basin in the man's cabin. It is no surprise that this girl admittedly hates women; having a child is the ugly punishment of being female. Deserted by the father of the child, she is left to care for the baby that issues from her like a foreign object and to confront the scorn of the community, in this most familiar plight of woman. With no compunction she murders the child, an act Oates does not repeat (although in some cases fathers murder their children). But if mothers do not kill their children, few of them have any helpful maternal concern for them.

Motherhood is a sinister concept in the literature of this period from almost any point of view, particularly when the mother takes overwhelming control. Oates's best characters are not her manipulating mothers, however. Natashya Everett, whom she satirizes in *Expensive People,* the mother Richard Everett kills for warping him into a monster, is supposedly everything the American woman wants to be; and the result is a great nothing. Clara Walpole, who for a time manipulates her son, is so shattered by her own fears that the boy is soon quite out of her control. From the lower-class woman's point of view, children, like sex, are simply another of the tangible and incomprehensible facts of life to be reckoned with as part of the economic burden. Fathers see children in much the same way. (The maniacal father of Jesse Harte in *Wonderland* slays everyone in his family except Jesse, who escapes, after a long period during which he is unemployed.)

As much as these women resent motherhood, however, few of them seem aware of any methods of birth control. Having a child is a dreaded inevitability. When Jules Wendall comes to his mother's place after her divorce from her second husband and sees another man at the table, he automatically expects another baby. (Mrs. Wendall is at the time taking care of one unwanted infant, the undesired result of her most recent marriage.) A child is often a threat to the sanity or to the lives of his parents. Oates has stated that her stories do not usually deal with the Oedipal theme because the fathers are not strong enough, but there is often a clear hint of it as one source of the violence—obviously so with Richard Everett's murder of his mother. Mothers may desire to kill their children, but they are usually too passive to take such decisive action.

Certainly one reason why mothers (young or middle-aged) are usually not shown to be manipulators is that from their point of view, and we see this through a female writer, they who feel incapable of ruling their own lives do not feel able to rule the lives of others. Mothers are afraid of their children as they watch them grow into separate beings whose nature they can never understand or control. The mother of two sons in "Extraordinary Popular Delusions" and Mrs. York in "Normal Love" believe that their children are not even aware of them. The motherly duties they perform mean nothing. Conscientious housewives often feel alien and trapped in their own homes, unable to understand why. They cannot make any sensible connection between the unasked-for attraction to the men they marry, the sexual act, which is usually treated as a dim memory, the children that result, their duties as housewives, and the strangers who are their husbands. Clara Walpole vividly recalls two facts about her mother's life: one night a man had climbed on top of her, and months later she died of it.

The dread of motherhood combines a woman's fears of men, among other things for causing pregnancy, and of children, both beyond her understanding and control. Like most male writers, Oates accepts the traditional roles of women. But where the male point of view suggests that motherhood should be a positive experience, Oates shows it only to be an awful one, as it brings to a climax the lifelong fears and hostilities her women have experienced. Their tensions erupt in some of the ugliest acts in her fiction.

A story simply called "The Children" consists of another of those smooth surfaces with a sinister underlying current which Oates creates so effectively. As graduate students, Ronald and Ginny marry, and she relinquishes her career with relief. Surprised to enjoy her move to the suburbs, she mingles with other wives, talking and acting as they do. The daughter born to her seems a perfect child, and for a time the mother's life passes in a comfortable blur as she considers herself in control. The concentration on others is a relief, for she may now define her life through the activities of her family. But as the beautiful, willful daughter grows, Ginny becomes increasingly frightened of her. A son is born, and young Rachel pokes at him to irritate her mother, telling her how the neighbors say she is a bad parent. The quiet afternoons in the suburbs gradually take on a nightmarish quality, and without understanding why, Ginny is terrified. Rachel keeps foreboding secrets from her, and at last the clash comes. Ginny beats her child wildly with a spoon, which is bloody by the time her husband comes home and takes it from her, as she screams at him, " 'Oh, *you* don't know! What do *you* know about it? What the hell do *you* know?' " "The Children" ranks with "Where Are You Going, Where Have You Been?" and "Normal Love" as one more superb account of the quiet terror women experience under "normal" circumstances.

In "The Children" hysteria breaks out early in the life of the young mother who beats her daughter, but the pattern is usually more prolonged and subtle, showing a gradual disintegration. Oates's works are everywhere informed by a fear of entropy—of things vanishing, wearing down, being torn away. Maureen Wendall is obsessed with the idea: "What would happen if everything broke into pieces? . . . How could you get hold of something that wouldn't end? Marriages ended. Love ended. Money could be stolen, found out and taken, Furlong himself might find it, or it might disappear by itself, like that secretary's notebook. Such things happened. Objects disappeared, slipped through cracks, devoured, kicked aside, knocked under the bed or into the trash, lost. Nothing lasted for long."

In "The Dead" an intelligent and successful young woman writer is shown in the fatal process of disintegration. In great demand as a speaker after the success of one of her novels, Ilena visits college campuses, satisfying the crowds who apparently see nothing strange in her condition, although she is heavily drugged. The story begins with the directions on a bottle of pills: "*Useful in acute and chronic depression, where accompanied by anxiety,*" an accurate diagnosis of Ilena's general condition. She is frightened all the time. But the doctor claims she is normal. When her husband is in the hospital she does not visit him once, "being hard of heart, like stone, and terrified of seeing him again. She feared his mother too." Her fears of sleep with its nightmares of Kennedy's assassination are one of the more obvious reminders of how the catastrophes of our times figure in our neuroses.

Ilena, one of the few professional and creative women to exist in this period of literature, is in even worse mental condition than most other women. Her novels are created out of her misery, and unlike the heavy physical work that keeps some women too occupied to go insane, her activity and awareness only feed the tensions that lead to insanity. She speaks fluently and intelligently, in the meantime fingering the pills in her pocket. Her teaching is either sluggish or hysterical, the two familiar sides of the same madness. Ilena is further split by taking a lover while she is married. But hers is not a problem of divided passion; she is simply exhausted by repeating the motions required of her body without the invigoration of true sexuality. She cannot live with two men. She cannot live with one. Oates has admitted her affinity with this intellectual type of person; and it is these people, she says, who are most given to violence, whether through the aggressive physical demonstrations of men or the insane and suicidal leanings of women. On the verge of suicide, Ilena gives an indifferent consent to marry again as a pattern of least resistance. In her madness the faces of men blend together, the only one standing out that of a student who died from an overdose of heroin. In her disintegration she imagines herself on a bed crammed with men merging into each other, becoming protoplasm. The snow falls as in Joyce's "The Dead," but it does not bring the peace of death for Ilena.

Since women never offer themselves to men for pleasure, of which they seem incapable, it is surprising in "The Sacred Marriage" to find a beautiful, gracious lady, widow of a famous poet, who immediately and happily goes to bed with the young instructor who visits her home to study her husband's papers—surprising, until we learn the real reason for her generous sexuality. After two weeks of cosy cohabitation with Howard Dean, his allotted time, Emilia greets a second scholar who has come for his turn with the precious papers and, it now becomes apparent, her bed that accompanies the project. Such easy lovemaking is indeed too good to be true. Dean discovers the answer in the author's papers, a short story of a famous novelist about to die who marries a beautiful woman so that she might pass on his divinity by taking a multitude of lovers. Thus Emilia is merely an agent. The male as the creator and the female who lives only through him form a version of the pattern found among less sophisticated Oatesian people for whom a man's relation to a woman is based on his physical and economic attributes rather than on creative achievements. In either case, women must have men to fill up their blankness. Men may be as dependent upon women to fill sexual and some emotional needs, but other things are also important to them: action, machinery, or, in this case, art. The best chance for a woman's healthy survival is for her not to resist her blankness but to succumb to it as Emilia does, or to develop the simple and fatalistic resilience of Loretta Botsford, mother of Maureen Wendall.

Most of the ideas important to women in Oates's fiction are brought together in Maureen. The frame for *them* is the claim that Maureen was one of the author's students, who wrote to her years after flunking her composition course, still disturbed by the discussions of form in literature and life which to her had nothing to do with the mess life really is. Oates states that she was so affected by the girl's story that she took it down in detail and presented it as a "work of history in fictional form," which she says is "the only kind of fiction that is real." The author's obvious affinity to this character is surely responsible in part for the novel's success. Maureen's anxieties, her anguish for having no fixed identity (which women seldom recognize in such an acute way), and the context of poverty are the materials that Oates works with best. Poverty and violence are not necessarily the sources of women's terror—Ilena's madness follows no such obstacles, and the quiet hysteria of Mrs. York, residing comfortably in the suburbs, is as acute as Maureen's. But her story powerfully combines fear of actual physical danger with anxiety for the subtle and the unknown. She is afraid of everything. "Asleep or awake I am afraid, and how can you live that way, always afraid? I am afraid of men out on the street if I see them or don't see them, I am afraid of cars hitting me, of people laughing at me, I am afraid of losing my purse, of throwing up in a store, of screaming out loud in the library and being kicked out and never allowed back."

Typically of Oates's novels, *them* opens with an announcement of violence: the teenage Loretta Botsford brings her young lover to her bed and is awakened the next morning by the sound of her brother shooting him in the head. Loretta's youth is over. She who the day before gazed frivolously at her own reflection and was pleased with its resemblance to a Hollywood image now dashes wildly into the street, half dressed, looking for the gun she realizes is necessary for survival in her neighborhood. The panic so clearly motivated in this early scene suggests a story that will keep us tied to the tangibles. The action is horrible, but we know exactly the source of Loretta's fears. In pragmatically closing her dreamy past as she takes up a gun to protect herself after her lover's death, Loretta proves to be one of the more fortunate women. She assumes no guilt, accepts events as inevitable, and then she acts.

Loretta lacks the deeper sensitivity that would allow her to see more, and fear more, as her daughter Maureen does. Loretta is, in fact, glad to be without a unique identity, the very thing her daughter desires: "She liked the fact that there were so many Lorettas, that she'd seen two girls in one week with a sailor outfit like her own, and a hundred girls with curly hair flung back over their shoulders!" This ability to be a blank on which a familiar copy might be impressed, whatever is popular at the time, keeps her from the great loneliness that is to plague Maureen as it plagues most people who are as self-consciously unusual as she.

In *them* men are outsiders either because they are at work or because they have left dreary domesticity for the excitement and profit they hope for in the random life of the city. Mama Wendall, the despised mother of Loretta's first husband, the policeman Howard Wendall, is a power-hungry old woman trying to head the matriarchy at home. She can control Maureen, who is easily affected by authority. But the younger sister Betty, a tough wench, has no qualms about shoving the old lady out the back door and kicking her down the steps. The strongest woman rules, not the oldest. Men may have control when they are at home, but since they are usually absent, women make up the lasting center of this life. Even the favored Jules is gradually lost to his family as the action centers on the women who remain at home.

Loretta is happier between husbands when she is working, gossiping, and going to movies, free for a time of pregnancy, than she is with a husband. Her addiction to Hollywood ideals brings her back to dreams of romantic love, but her marriages have no resemblance to such dreams. Children come as part of the unromantic reality, but she likes them, nevertheless, and they like her, perhaps because she is too fatalistic to believe she can manipulate them. What has she to do with the creation and control of the mysterious Maureen? Loretta is often thoughtless with her daughter, rousing the girl from sleep in order to use her bed to escape a fight with her husband. And Maureen is forced to take care of her violent stepfather Furlong, a contact which leads to a murderous attack on her. But Loretta is no bitch mother whose determination is to mold her children's identity. She leaves Maureen with the burden of housework but allows her to do it her own way. This mother is so vulnerable that the daughter is never given an illusion of perfection, which is often the weapon of a manipulating mother. Maureen is baffled because her mother does not love her more, but she pities her and fears the consequences of her haphazard life.

Loretta escapes with a few beers every afternoon and the fellowship of women like herself. Maureen has no such escape—her solitary hours in the library only lead to disturbing thoughts. Loretta has never had either the inclination or the capacity for such contemplation. Her fantasies, and they are rather ordinary ones, make up only a small part of her life. Even as a teenager in the spell of Hollywood she worked six days a week in a laundry before emerging for one Saturday night as a star. Such a proportion of pleasure to drudgery is an accurate estimation of what her experiences are to be, but for her the general heaviness of life only increases the pleasure of its few satisfactions. Oates, who has been accused of eliminating the possibilities of life's delights, has not made existence completely dismal for Loretta. She gets a crude enjoyment from unloading the groceries as if they were special prizes for her children. Such delight is not meant to romanticize the economic and spiritual poverty of the Wendalls but to show the person who will thrive best in such a condition.

Maureen, Loretta's second-born after her favorite child Jules, is a strangely diligent daughter. She cleans up after the others, and her half of the bedroom is noticeably the neat half. But her silence and withdrawal from the rest of the family make them suspicious of her and reluctant to accept her as one of them. Sometimes she reveals a hatred of her confinement and occasionally of her entire family, but much stronger than rebellion is her desire to fit in somewhere and to be safe. Maureen is angry and hard without being a fighter. Above all, she desires form and control. Not wishing to destroy, she is forced to live in the midst of destructive forces.

One of the most memorable things about Maureen is the lustful way she hoards her money between the pages of a book of poetry. We might ask why this cautious and intelligent girl never puts her money in the bank, for it is painfully obvious that it will be discovered or stolen if she leaves it in her room. But the actual touch of money is important to her. The one greatest pleasure in her life is to be alone with her bills, which are so sacred to her that she will not even count them and reduce them to a mere numerical value. Her possibilities of escape to a job and a place of her own are so remote that the money in her hand is all she can believe in.

Maureen makes this money through prostitution. An unnamed man picks her up after school each day, and they go to a motel where she passively allows him to make love to her (while all she thinks of is the payment she is about to receive). Like Oates's other women, she is without sexual response. She never asks her client, who remains dim to us because she has no interest in him, about his work or his family. While prostitution is often shown as a sordid, perverted, or even an erotic experience for a woman, here it is simply a means to an end, not desirable, not terrible, not even memorable. It is simply *the* way for a woman to get money, which is almost always the property of men. Maureen's family keep up a pretense to a strong taboo against any loose dealings between men and women, and Mrs. Wendall appears to be shocked that her daughter could be anything but a "nice" girl. But she did her time as a prostitute quite as easily as

Maureen does, when she first came to Detroit as the penniless mother of three children.

Sexual experience under such circumstances is a relatively unimportant event in a girl's life, except as it brings money. Maureen's lack of feeling is the most striking thing about her activities as a prostitute. The sex act is swiftly passed over, apparently making little impression on the woman. No foreplay here. The act of sex often merely announces that a child will be born, accompanied by none of the explicit detail that marks a discussion of it in most contemporary fiction. And to the women of *them*, burdened with the practical, the idea of love is as remote as other elements in the lives of the rich, who are considered to possess it as one of their luxuries. Only Jules has a romantic notion of love, which he dramatically lives out in his affair with Nadine Green (who later tries to kill him). Maureen does not even understand the fantasies of romantic love. To her teacher she addresses the pathetic question, " 'But how do you fall in love?' "

While Maureen may not fantasize about love or sexual pleasure, the thought of sexual assault with its threat of mutilation and murder is an unspoken but primary source of fear, as it is elsewhere in Oates's fiction. While Maureen's inner life is shown in quite extensive detail with little attention to rape, this may be because it is too nightmarish a thought to bring to the surface often. Only in one of her few moments of relative safety—she is under the hair dryer between her mother and a friend who comfortably gossip—does she dare openly consider things that ordinarily frighten her: "A girl dragged into a car not two blocks away and raped and pushed out the door, ending up half dead, and the girl was someone Maureen knew." She is not obsessed with an irrational fear. She simply knows what can happen and is understandably afraid.

When Maureen's stepfather discovers her money (and knows immediately how she got it), he almost kills her. The attack puts her in a comatose condition that lasts thirteen months, a period in which all she does is grow fat, one of the Oatesian woman's bizarre responses to her disgust with men and with her life in general. Maureen's long lapse from sanity pushes the traditional passivity of the woman to an extreme: she simply lies in bed and becomes a very large vegetable. Unlike Jules, who lashes out in his frustration, Maureen, the "good girl," turns her miseries in upon herself, giving up the struggle and assimilating death in her catatonic condition.

Maureen's life is guided by a fear that operates much as it does for the Kafka character who considers himself a guilty stranger. (During one period of her life, Oates says she felt she *was* Kafka.) In those lofty edifices which call forth Maureen's respect, such as the library, she is particularly intimidated and afraid. She always feels herself in the wrong in the presence of authority. When the librarian blames her for the torn page in her library book, proving it could not have been ripped when the book was checked out, Maureen believes her. She borrows a quarter from Jules to pay for the damaged book, without telling him why, acting as desperate as one who has committed a severe crime. She does well at school until she loses the notebook of class records when she is the homeroom secretary. Oates says that this is the worst thing that ever happens to Maureen. Her responsibility is more important to her than any she is ever to have, and such a failure is stunning. The nun in charge of the class sternly advises her to keep looking for the notebook, but the search along city streets is hopeless. This is one of those horribly conclusive experiences it is possible to have when you are young that have the power of suggesting the way things will always be, an event more profound to Maureen than even the murder of Loretta's lover is to her.

But if Maureen is merely paranoid, the reader is far too convinced of the real destructive potential in her life to consider her so. At home her stepfather lustfully approaches her and finally beats her. Where can she be safe? One of the visitors to her home is her Uncle Brock, Loretta's brother who murdered her lover several years before. Maureen's fears arise from contact with such tangible evidence of violence, and her statements often have the flat, unemotional, but uncontroversial quality of fact. Her fear is cold, certain, and pervasive, but it seldom breaks into the hysteria that would threaten herself or others, for she also operates under a pressure to control herself and to achieve, which is usually the curse of the more affluent child. Maureen's particular misfortune is to suffer both the threats of actual violence and the anxieties for real and imagined harm to come from the forces of authority lurking everywhere.

The most likeable one of them is Jules, whose freedom of movement and capacity for romanticizing his love affairs is a pleasant contrast to Maureen's sense of entrapment. Jules is every bit as desperate as Maureen, and he comes to lead a more disastrous life than hers. But his is at least enlivened by greater energy and choice. A comparison of this brother and sister make the particular fears and responses of a woman more noticeable. The differences between them could be merely the quirks of two personalities, but too much arises from their roles as man and woman to ignore.

Jules was always a daring child, frightened of nothing and soon known as the troublemaker who set the barn on fire when he first learned to strike a match. His grandmother predicts that he will die in the electric chair, a prediction to be repeated precisely by others throughout his life. When we last see Jules he has killed a policeman. But he manages to remain lovable all along, adored by the mother and sister he continues to care for and send money to whenever he can. He becomes a thief in behalf of his girlfriend Nadine, taking a car so they can escape together. Each night from their motel rooms across the country he steals supper for her as conscientiously as another man might bring home his paycheck. Nadine remains an icy, sadistic, although fairly unconvincing character, a stimulant for Jules's crime, spurred on by his wildness but scornful of his talk of love.

Jules goes far out to Texas, while Maureen remains ensconced in her room. She pleads for a chance to go to work, but the excuse is that she is needed at home. A job is as remote to her as are other desirable, untouchable prizes somewhere outside. Surely this is one reason why she hoards her money, while Jules is generous with his. One of his companions observes that women " 'don't understand where money comes from or what it means or how a man can be worth money though he hasn't any at the moment.' " Women know only that men have the money, and that is where they must get it. Jules appreciates this same principle to the extent that he feels it his duty to somehow provide things for Nadine and his mother. To capture a special girl like Nadine Green he believes he needs a million.

Maureen goes back to school a few years after her recovery from Furlong's beating, and the following months of inactivity, a thinner and more determined person. Her schooling does not open her to experience, however, but serves as a means of new protection. She now attends carefully to the face and figure that will capture the appropriate man, someone she thinks will make life safe by giving her a house and children. Her gentle, married instructor, father of three children, will do. Maureen's success in taking this man from his wife is not entirely credible, but she is correct in seeing him as a person so worried by one failure in marriage that he would not have the nerve to leave a second wife. The deliberate act of taking another woman's husband is carried out in much the same amoral way as is Maureen's earlier act of prostitution. It is incongruous but believable that this girl's conscience, which could be blown out of proportion by the slightest infringement of the rules as a child (e.g., her experience in the library), could be blotted out this way later on. Her pragmatic plan of survival succeeds, but with a totally narrowing effect.

Perhaps taking a married man is Maureen's only way of bypassing the romantic stages between men and women that she never believed in or understood anyway and getting on to the tangible results of husband and house which are her goal. In a letter to her teacher (presumably Joyce Carol Oates) she admits that she could not divulge the plan of taking another woman's husband to a married woman, who would obviously not want someone to steal her husband, although she suspects that her teacher might not mind taking someone else's husband if the story were pretty enough. But she needs someone to know of her greatest success. And yet as we last see her nervously closing the door on her brother Jules after a brief, whispered conversation with him, the person she had cared for more than anyone else, we know that her life is closing. She may have mastered certain surface elements of her life by obtaining a husband and some financial security, but in turning away her brother she shows how numbed she is to any truly lifegiving responses.

Oates is deadly accurate with Maureen and others like her whose dread she makes vivid. Her women treated only satirically are not as successful. The Nada of *Expensive People* is never quite present (as her son and husband discover). The too obvious allusion to nothingness and the catalogs of products that make up her life may document the malaise of the expensive people, but they do not give us a real woman. And Maureen Wendall is that. The fears of poverty with its accompanying physical violence, as well as the quiet terror created by the powers that rule, are impressively true. And no one is better at showing the female consciousness aware of the possibilities of rape than Joyce Carol Oates. She is a master at depicting women's anxieties of many sorts, and she makes a striking contribution to our understanding of contemporary America as seen by women. Here is an author to read if one dares to know the particular fear there is in being a woman— here and now—even when the surface of life may appear as familiar and safe as a supermarket on a sunny day.

ROSE MARIE BURWELL

With Shuddering Fall
and the Process of Individuation

Although it has taken reviewers and critics more than a decade to recognize that Joyce Carol Oates is not writing in the mode of the naturalist or the social realist, her first novel introduces the search for self-realization that provides the narrative structure of all Oates's fiction. The true subject of *With Shuddering Fall* is not, as reviewers assumed it to be, madness or violence. It is the complex drive of the human organism toward psychological wholeness which Jung terms individuation, and here Oates holds in uneasy tension the entelechy of personal individuation and the psychologically entrenched power of those institutions which impede it.

Written while the novelist was an undergraduate, the first novel resembles, in many of the perceptions of the two major characters, "The Myth of Sisyphus" as it might be recreated by an autistic high school drop-out— exactly the developmental stage of protagonist Karen Herz. With her racing-car driver lover, Shar Rule, Karen participates in a drama suggesting the extremes to which existential recognition of self-responsibility leads. The structure of the tripartite novel originates in the psychic condition of Karen before, during and after her moral maturation. The short first section takes place in Eden County, the mythical territory in which the second novel and many of the early short stories are set. It reveals Karen in a quiescent, but restless, moral state. The long middle section has as its background the racing circuit towns of Synderdale and Cherry River, presenting the emotional and physical violence with which, for Oates, the self is inevitably

From *Canadian Literature*, no. 73 (Summer 1977). © 1977 by the University of British Columbia, Vancouver.

created. The brief final section returns to Eden County; leaving ambiguous, but achievable, a consolidation of the moral independence to which Karen aspires.

As the structure of the novel derives from Karen's moral states, so does the psychology of her character originate in a mnemonic pattern through which reduplicated scenes force her to confront the emotional price of moral dependence. In much the way as the bit of tea-soaked madeleine evokes for Proust's Marcel elements of the past which create a new reality in the present, Karen re-experiences humiliation and suffering and is strengthened in her nascent desire to seize control of her life. Waking on the morning of what, unknown to her, is the day that she will leave Eden County, Karen forces herself up and out of the deep, protective slumber that has immured her since birth—giving to the life where her destiny is shaped by the family and its traditions a dream-like quality. The previous night she had listened to her father reading of the biblical patriarchs whose destinies were manipulated by God himself and had felt keenly the lure of such surety. Karen recalls the visit to a dying neighbour on which she recently accompanied her father. Even when she was a small child, the hermit, Old Rule, had inspired awe in her: she had feared touching the rock that was his seat by the creek. Now his impending death awakens in her a sense of both dread and anticipation. In his junk-filled sickroom, several days ago, Karen was seized with terror at the sight of a trap protruding from beneath his bed. She senses inchoately that he is linked with an unknown destiny that awaits her apart from her existence as the pampered youngest daughter of a back-country patriarch.

Before the day ends, Rule's son, Shar, has given Karen a glimpse of that destiny. Shar is thirty; brutal and surly, he has been recalled by his dying father to the hills he fled fourteen years earlier. Accustomed to taking what he wants, and fascinated by the pale golden beauty of Karen who was three years old when he left Eden County, Shar deceives her into accompanying him on an errand. Though Shar has presupposed an innocence in Karen that will necessitate sexual coercion, he unknowingly becomes the tool, and ultimately the victim, of a force compared to which his carnal obsession is whimsy. Karen resists his advances, yet the idea of returning home creates hysteria in her. Seizing the steering wheel, she causes an auto crash that foreshadows, even in the imagery of its voluptuousness, the track smash-up in which Shar will die. The crash triggers a violent confrontation between Karen's father and Shar. As Old Rule's body burns in the cabin his son has ignited, the two battle before it—an encounter that for Karen quite literally ends the old rule and further awakens her from moral somnolence.

Since Karen's earliest memories Shar has symbolized a dark and forbidden world, unknowable to her as the protected daughter of the community's largest landowner:

> Now, a man of thirty, Shar belonged to neither world—not the dim, safe past or the static present . . . he had always been on the periphery of their lives—despised and admired by the children themselves. . . . he now revealed himself as a creature of another species, a stranger. Karen had felt watching her father and Shar at supper . . . a sense of warning, of something unavoidable they must—together—defeat.

On the day he returned to Eden County, Shar had reminded Karen of "a hawk, a bird of prey that circled the skies." Now, watching her father's futile efforts to force Shar backward into the burning cabin, as though he were driving a demon back into hell, Karen knows that her anticipated destiny is embodied in this struggle. She murmurs, "Never the same again!"

Even as she stands over her father, who has been knocked to the ground by Shar, and hears his command, "Karen—Get him. Don't come to me until you get him. Kill him. Kill him," Karen recognizes her complicity in the action:

> Karen felt that, deep inside, secretly . . . she was able to think clearly and sanely. The fault did indeed lie in her, was of her doing: but it originated not in the decision to go with Shar but in her deliberately resisting sleep that morning. That was so—she had pushed against sleep, pushing herself up out of it as though she were moving slowly up through water to the clean air above . . . Perhaps she had understood, without really being able to know, that the rejection of her child's bed would lead, after a series of insane, vivid scenes, to the picture of her father lying in the cold mud, bleeding . . . how right he was to judge her, to find her guilty!

Although Karen accepts the fact that in willing herself to awake from the dream of childhood she is guilty of her father's injury, and although she pursues Shar as her father commands, finally dictating his death, the recognition of Oates's use of incrementally important memories reveals that Karen's actions derive not from her father's command, but from a force toward self-determination that is hers alone.

The scene before the burning cabin takes place in a context that seems unreal to Karen, like a dream or a nightmare. But as she begins to pursue

Shar, her head is clear. These are images of a dichotomy incrementally associated with the struggle to free existence from chance that is the novel's thematic centre. What happens as the result of unthinking acceptance of the cycles established by family, church or nature occurs in the state of dream, fog, insanity or nightmare and is *accident* to the individual who has not reflected and chosen. What happens as the result of sanity or clarity of vision or choice is *freedom*. Karen, significantly, integrates the content of the unconscious, making it a conscious choice when she gives herself to Shar. Following him through the woods, while her father lies unconscious, she ponders, "if this was not a dream it was closely related to a dream— surely she had dreamed of a man in this wood, a man in any of the woods, awaiting her."

Mnemonic motivation continues as Karen pursues Shar across the frozen terrain of Eden County: the memory which overpowers her is of an incident from her childhood in which she made a moral choice at great cost. She had shocked and offended a male teacher who pruriently sought the details of what boys had done to her on the playground:

> "Tell me what he does," the teacher said.
> "He does this!" Karen said impatiently. She pulled the skirt of her dress up and stared at the teacher's alarmed look. "I'm not ashamed of anything," she said, letting the skirt fall back . . . "Now you leave me alone too!" Even in the face of the knowledge that she would be completely alone at school after this, she could not help but feel a sense of bitter joy . . . In spite of her anger she knew somehow that she had done right, and that the teacher, shaken and ashamed, recognized it.

Now, pleading silently for the forgiveness of her father, whose rule she has abandoned in order to further forge her own moral universe, Karen follows Shar into the rat-infested barn where they make love. On the penultimate page of the novel, Karen, who has suffered a psychic collapse after Shar's death, analyzes the alternatives now open to her in what doctors call her "self-cured" state. She realizes that in this initiation lay the germ of Shar's death:

> I can accuse him [her father] of my own crime and guilt and with enough hysteria I can convince myself that I had no part in what I did—that the filthy way that strange man made love to me the first time had nothing to do with that man's death.

Together Karen and Shar leave Eden County. Shar, who denies any responsibility for the confrontation with Herz, asserting, "it isn't the end of anything . . . It's only now begun." When the mid-section of the novel opens, two and one-half months later, Shar has just begun to comprehend the meaning of his own disclaimer. Gradually he is being forced out of the moral passivity from which Karen arose on the morning of the day he struck her father. Here, in the racing-circuit towns of Synderdale and Cherry River, the two undergo the violent moral maturation that assigns to Shar the fulfillment of the novel's strange title and creates in Karen a consciousness which will ultimately transcend the knowledge that is its content. The title comes from Meredith's "Ode to the Spirit of Earth in Autumn," suggesting in its rhetorical context the positive and consummative nature of Shar's death:

> Death shall I shrink from, loving thee?
> Into the breast that gives the rose,
>   Shall I with shuddering fall?

In Synderdale Oates introduces Max, Shar's sponsor, a bloated, voyeuristic entrepreneur who would be psychopomp to Karen and Shar though his own existence exemplifies a moral stance diametrically opposite theirs. Max, whose name, given its German pronunciation—mocks—indicates his moral callousness, insists he is arbiter of ethical responsibility while insulating himself from accountability by self-deception, over-indulgence, hypochondria and pseudo-piety. Impotent, Max has vicariously shared Shar's willingly recounted sexual exploits for fourteen years—inhibiting moral awareness in the younger man to nourish his own lust for omnipotence and omniscience. Like the gods whom Sisyphus affronted, Max has robbed Shar (and would rob Karen) of his dignity by assuming responsibility for his actions. When Shar realizes that in leaving Eden County he had not escaped one mode of life for another, but merely traded his legal father for Max, he recognizes Max as an aspect of that imago in which Karen had perceived Old Rule—as a rock protruding from a creek. Such figures always create obstacles around which the life of the individual, if it is not to be dammed or diverted, must cut its own channel. The image also reflects, albeit unconsciously, the authority of the Church—the rock which, for Karen (and socio-historically), is inextricably linked to the authority of the father. But as the gods underestimated Sisyphus, so is Max wrong in his assessment of Karen and Shar. He speaks of them as innocent, incapable of sin, brutal, clever children, full of life and destined for a long life—asserting that for them all things are accidents. However, when Shar forces an opponent into a flaming crash which Max calls an accident, Karen insists in cold anger, "Not all things are accidents." On the evening of the track "accident," Max sits in a country tavern with Shar, Karen and other racing-circuit people. In a scene infused with perverse sexuality, he re-lives Shar's violent triumph:

> Max sat with his back to the wall so that he could see everything that went on in the crowded place. He ate melons luxuriously: pale green melons, smooth as skin, that the waiter—a boy of about seventeen—kept bringing him. Seeds had spilled out onto the table and on the front of his shirt, though he did not seem to notice. He waved the big glistening knife at them as he spoke . . . "A woman's love is a beautiful thing to see," Max went on, licking at a sudden rivulet of juice that ran down his chin. "She is transformed by it, absolutely transformed. That has never been part of my experience" . . . With a flourish Max finished his melon and took a deep breath and called for the waiter. "Another one of these," he said, sighing helplessly. The table was wet with juice and scattered seeds that the boy—a rushed, alarmed-looking country boy with long hair—did not offer to wipe up, "You must tell me how the race was for you," Max said, laying a damp hand on Shar's arm.

As Max leaves the tavern with Karen (Shar remains behind with another woman), he recoils in fear from a small boy holding a snake. The reptile incorporates for Max the universal principal of evil which he would deny, and in its phallic signification, the humiliation of his own impotence.

Max posits for Karen an innocence that protects her from suffering and urges her to abandon any hope of finding meaning in existence: "Your life is not a metaphor for anything else," he coaxes; "it ends when you do." In his self-deception, Max, whom Karen once speculates might have devoured Shar, fails to understand that it is exactly the certainty of death which impels the individual to search for meaning in life, and failing to find it in traditional forms and institutions, to create it within the confines of free will. As Karen's attraction to Shar grows, she begins to sense the threat it poses to her freedom: waiting in a shabby room for him to come to her, she contemplates the possibility that the passive resistance which has defined her intactness thus far may not be enough. Against the force of such passion, it may eventually have to yield to an act of violence.

Because Max considers himself alone capable of moral contemplation, his miscalculations are immense. In his blind omniscience he pontificates that Shar functions not consciously, but viscerally: Shar from the stomach and Karen (because it seems more delicate to him) from the heart. Ironically,

Karen, whose last name means heart in German, has earlier made the bitter decision to harden her heart, to render herself pitiless. On the night of the melon-eating incident Karen had lain in a hotel room, knowing as the hours passed that Shar was with another woman, and had resolved to resist "a universe that contrived her life in order that she might be here tonight in this dirty hotel room alone, waiting." Staring at the shape of a giant cockroach formed by a water stain on the ceiling, Karen concludes:

> If some men supposed themselves free it was only because they did not understand that they were imprisoned, bars could be made of any dreamy loss of light.

Max's doctor offers her sleeping pills, but Karen refuses, "If there was pain, she would feel it; it was hers." Falling asleep, she dreams of a child who has been growing inside a dusty closet where bright summer dresses hang—a child with plastic veins and a plastic heart. And she resolves not to cry for the death of that child, not to project meaning or seek comfort where none exists:

> Better to look into an empty drawer, stare into an empty hole, than to discover oneself looking into a darkness filled with shape.

Although Karen's dream, in incorporating her assent to the death of a child, foreshadows her desire for the miscarriage that will free her of Shar's baby, it is more significant in the narrative as a miniaturization of the dilemma in which she is enmeshed. Childhood is essentially a stultifying and confining condition, no matter how diverting and beautiful. Emergence involves, by definition, giving up the protection of the closet, the brightness of the summer dresses. Karen's resolution not to mourn the death of the child is a recognition and an acceptance of the pain inherent in the personal transformation toward which she moves. Significantly, the material from the unconscious, revealed in the dream, is incorporated in her deliberate actions later in the same way that in giving herself to Shar the first time she chose what she had earlier dreamed. On the day that she sends Shar to his death, Karen's memory of her suffering this night, and the hardening of heart to which it led her, is triggered by another cockroach shape on a wall.

Because Shar has become habituated to avoiding responsibility, his moral maturation must inevitably be more violent than Karen's. As the words *dream, fog, nightmare* and *insanity* are associated with Karen when her destiny is out of her own control, so the words *victim, desperate, blind, trapped* and *possessed* now characterize Shar. Unlike Karen, who assumes the existence of a universal force she must resist, Shar believes his birth to have been an accident. On the racing circuit, where all his adult life has been spent, Shar has never needed to commit himself beyond the physical act—on the track or in bed. This fact has heretofore been a source of pride to him: now, with Karen, who withholds herself even in union, he feels trapped. Reading the newspapers over and over, he hopes that Karen's father will come for her, relieving him of the choice. Like Max, Shar at first deceives himself: he thinks that he controls Karen, that she echoes his statements and has no existence apart from him. At the same time he suffers from the knowledge of his own loss of control. Shar's last name seems, like Karen's, to function signally and ironically, for he struggles fatally to attain rule or control of his own destiny.

Shar's first step toward the moral premeditation which produces the Nietzschean self-overcoming of the novel's epigraph ("What is done out of love always take place beyond good and evil") is his imperfect awareness that in relation to Karen he feels "enchanted, desperate and incomplete." He is bewildered because, for the racer—the role in which he has until now found his identity—danger comes not from giving in to the inside, but from being drawn off centre by centrifugal force. Since he has dealt with Karen only as an extension of himself, Shar, who hungers for a communion with her and with the crowd that comes to see him race, does not yet know that for the individual whose existence is deliberate, the centre of being controls *all* actions. Only thus does one achieve the limited communion possible for man in the exile that is existence. It is in the condition of calculated action, which finally replaces accident in his life, that Shar embraces death as a transcendence—fulfilling the novel's title. Karen calls Shar's creation of his own death his manhood.

Neither brutality nor indifference can accomplish Shar's desired mastery over Karen. Their lovemaking becomes a battle of wills: in a terrible coupling where Shar takes her by force in a cemetery, Karen dominates—putting their actions into the realm of a dream, absolving herself, by an act of will, from any need to control what is happening to her body. At the instant of consummation, Karen looks—clear-eyed—into Shar's face. He is impaled, furious; even as the orgasm seizes him, he slaps her, sobbing:

> "Look at me like that, you little bitch!" . . . His face was white. . . . "I'd like to set you on fire like I did to *him*," he said, "take a match and set you on fire—burn everything—your clothes catching on and burning—you screaming for help, you little

bitch! And all burning up, hair and insides, so you could see inside and see things burning there, melting away, burning—."

In his desire to burn Karen, Shar reveals that the love/hate bond between them, which for Karen is the result of a nascent urge toward moral maturation, is as yet not different to him than his previous relationships—on the race track and in bed. In response to Karen's resistance Shar would like to invoke his habitual mode of violence as he had done in forcing his racing opponent into the flaming crash. Karen's response is diametrically opposite: She contracts herself into a "tiny pebble-like thing, safe in her brain." In his research in strivings toward psychic wholeness and in his analysis of mandala symbolism Jung found that a conflict rendered into images of stone is a positive human attitude toward the process of transformation. For the person undergoing the individuation the unity of the imagined stone is a projection of the unified self toward which he strives. For Shar this defeat-in-victory of the deathly union in the cemetery provides the energy for his first step toward moral maturation: when Karen awakens the following morning he is gone. She is incredulous, for she had thought him "trapped, incapable of playing the game, unaware of its rules."

Tired, sick with the child that (unknown to Shar) is growing inside her, Karen is tempted to abandon the pursuit of a deliberate existence which must now, because she is obsessed with him, include Shar's death. She considers Max's offer of an abortion arrangement and one thousand dollars in return for her going home, but such a bargain would leave Shar alive and the terrible attraction that threatens her freedom still viable. Contemplating this, Karen cries, "I am lost, I am lost," and once again the necessity of creating whatever meaning her life is to have is strengthened mnemonically as she re-experiences a childhood agony:

> She found herself thinking, inexplicably, as she sometimes did when Shar made love to her, of scenes of her childhood . . . she had not thought of for years. The proud pony one of the boys had ridden to school that time—why did she remember it now . . . How she had wanted a pony like that! How she had cried for it, crawling about her father's knees! "But why didn't he ever get it for me?" . . . She was struck by her father's queer injustice. She felt she could not forgive him that.

Karen's memory is of an injustice, a betrayal. Significantly, betrayal is also the emotion Karen associates with being swept up in passion for Shar. Now she resists the temptation to return to a life in which happiness can be withheld by another. Following Shar to Cherry River, she materializes before him as out of a dream.

Leaving Karen in Synderdale was Shar's first step in personal transformation, and like Sisyphus discovering the absurd he experiences happiness in his heightened awareness of the limitations to which his existence is subject. The seed of knowledge that he now shares with Karen—that the individual must create his own destiny with an existence bounded by death—begins to expand within him. He tells his relief driver, "For them [the cars' owners] it's money and for me, waiting to die." And, as the sea and the sun take on great value for Sisyphus when he is commanded to return to the underworld, misanthropic Shar experiences a strange joy in his surroundings, "A damn good world! I can't get close enough to it—" he mutters. With this glimpse of joy inherent in his own freedom (and its attendant responsibility) Shar's life takes on a new complexity: he can no longer love and hate simply and immediately. Like Karen, he has left behind, in the world of his moral childhood, such clear distinctions. His life, like hers, will never again be the same. Now he contemplates the symbiotic relationship with Max which has relieved him of moral accountability—and moral freedom—his entire adult life. Like Karen who had rejected Max's settlement and returning to Eden County with "I am lost, I am lost," Shar thinks of Max and feels, for an instant, as if he were lost. And, just as Karen had done on the days immediately before leaving home, Shar surveys the world around him and wonders if he is insane. Karen, who survives Shar, will conclude that it *is* insane to look for meaning in existence—*and insane not to.*

The two women with whom Shar passes time in Cherry River occupy moral positions which contrast with that taken several months ago by Karen and now tentatively, reluctantly, embraced by the awakening Shar. Miriam, a big, slack Italian girl, contemplates the horror of rape/mutilation murders and freak shows with a morbid, unquestioning curiosity, "calmly and without much interest." She is both a foil for Karen and a facet of Shar's former self, insensitive and unspeculative. After a night together they both have "white, brutal faces, pleased with each other." Miriam's passive acceptance of existence is conveyed powerfully by her reaction to a carnival freak show. She delights in the grotesque novelty of the Siamese twins suspended in alcohol and insists on watching a race among the armless, legless freaks. The carnival barker cries:

Bo, Terry, Little Jo—here they are, just as they were born. They don't want your sympathy folks . . . they take their fate as it is, they accept their condition. They don't question the ways of our Maker and so why should we?

But Shar has begun to question. He cannot bear the sight: "Let's get the hell out of here," he moans. Miriam stays.

The second girl, a hostess whom Max sends to distract Shar before the race, is significantly nameless. She takes on an identity to please whatever man she is with and speaks of herself in passive voice, "it was thought best for me . . . I was told . . . it was decided." Shar quickly recognizes that Max has chosen her because she is "a pale, bloodless parody of Karen."

Shar can neither return to the state in which Max absolves him of moral responsibility nor establish a relationship with the girls contrasted to Karen. Karen cannot accept the payoff Max offers and return home. For each a resumption of the old way would mean loss of the awakening self. And so they pursue the collision course which must result in the death of one. Karen uses the money Max gives her not for an abortion, but to follow Shar. Encountering her on the street, Shar leads Karen directly to his shabby room where he takes her with a simple violence that he believes will purge the emotion which overpowers him—"He did not know if it was anger or lust or joy," expecting from it a communion that will release him. He finds instead, betrayal. The pregnancy, unknown to Shar until Karen begins to miscarry, further disarms him. It has been a mock communion, but through it Shar realizes that, bad as existence is, *he* makes the choices that determine it: " 'A hell of a world,' Shar said suddenly and self-consciously, 'but at least it's my own fault.' " Moved as he has never been before, Shar begs Karen to stay, to marry him. Although it is a plea she has longed to hear, although she has just acknowledged her love for him, in the centre of Karen's consciousness remains the knowledge that capitulation would again put her destiny in the hands of another. Again memory intervenes—this time in the form of a delirious dream which links Shar with her father and the distress of childhood dependency:

> While Shar sat by the window and watched her, Karen was having a dream. She was running through grass, up the slope before her home to join her father; his face when he embraced her was always rough . . . She was going to cry to him that it was done, everything was finished, clean, she had come home, but when he gripped her she shrank suddenly in size and the air turned hot and humid . . . She was seized by him—how young she was!—and she realized then that someone else had held her, . . . Shar—it must have been Shar . . . But when she turned,

the dream ended; she saw nothing. She grated her teeth in anger
and dismay.

Once again incorporating the content of the unconscious which has come
forward in the dream, Karen makes the extreme existential decision—that
there is no fate which cannot be overcome by contempt. She says, in the
calm, ordinary voice she had so despised in her sister, "You make me
sick."

Once again Shar's reaction is rendered in terms aligning him with
Sisyphus: both exert their whole being and accomplish nothing. For Shar, as
for Sisyphus, the lucidity that constitutes the torture also crowns the victory.
Going directly from Karen's sickbed to the track, he experiences a surge of
joy and love for the world, for Mitch his black assistant and for the crowd
who he knows comes to see him die. In recognizing that the communion of
violence the crowd seeks in the race, like the communion of sexual possession he sought with Karen, is a mockery, Shar knows that he has been
transformed:

> Shar's heart pounded with the excitement that he finally tran-
> scended the fragments of his anonymity. He wanted to get out
> and run back to Mitchie, or to Max, and explain to him: he
> knew who he was, he knew exactly what he was doing, and why;
> he was guilty—completely guilty—and his guilt, like his love,
> had pulled him together.

Karen has always known who she is; now Shar is also certain of his identity
and in the transcendence made possible by choice, he accepts death: he
hates the helmet, the fireproof suit he must wear—they are shock ab-
sorbers that disguise his humanity, devices invented for safety's sake—"as
if there were any possible protection against mortality." This realiza-
tion *is* Shar's psychic synthesis, his individuation. Pushing the traction
limit of his racer to the invisible point at which control turns to chaos, he
embraces death.

Karen has made a choice which will plunge her into a less final death—
the madness that Oates calls the suicide of cowards. As Shar leaves her
room, Karen masters a powerful urge to call him back:

> She wanted him back, she did not care what he had done—She
> struggled out of bed . . . Her blood pounding so furiously that
> she could not see . . . Her vision cleared. She was staring across
> the corridor at something—it drew her gaze like a magnet. A fat
> cockroach crawling precariously up the wall . . . Her mind was

emptied . . . She did not call after Shar. After a minute she realized she was listening to nothing, that he had left.

Memory has again kept Karen on the course of self-determination, for the
cockroach she sees here, with terrible clarity of vision, conjures up the
cockroach-shaped stain on the ceiling of the room in Synderdale and with it,
the bitter suffering inherent in a state where happiness can be withheld by
another. The hardness of heart Karen had resolved to maintain serves her
well: she does not call Shar back.

The short final segment of the novel traces the five months of Karen's
breakdown and recovery. She has known the extremes of abandonment of
the self to the family and to religious ecstasy and she has known the self-
containment which makes even love a threat to be met with violent resistance. Now she reaches a balance between hope and despair. Her physician
calls her "self-cured." Returning to her father's house in early December,
Karen enters again the morally somnolent world where the cycles of nature
and the liturgical calendar inure one to unquestioning acceptance of the
moral absolutes they symbolize. Parishioners who observe Karen at mass
with her family interpret her pain-marked countenance as proofs of the
justice of their universe, unable to comprehend that she has suffered only
because either way amounts to the same thing—it is insane to try to make
sense of existence, and insane not to.

Karen knows, as Shar knew at the moment of his death, that no real
communion is possible in life, a knowledge that allows her to choose the
conformity that will unite her—as much as she can ever be united—with
those who do not try to make sense of existence. She resolves to receive the
sacrament with them the following week, but to protect herself from the
thin splendour of church ritual which stands eternally ready to absolve her
of individuality. She retains the terrible clarity of vision that impelled her to
leave Eden County, to reject Shar and now to return home: Kneeling slowly,
"Karen . . . forced her mind to stay clear." Of the alternatives now open to
her, none is threatening for she concludes that whatever she becomes will be
of her own doing.

Karen's final evaluation of her circumstances can be seen in the reor-
dering of her vision of nature in Eden County. As the sense of an independent destiny grew within her last April she thought:

> In the worst days of winter the snow looked like an incredible
> sifting of earth and heaven, blotting out both earth and heaven,
> reducing them to an insane struggle of white that struck at hu-
> man faces like knives. Summers reeked with heat and heaven

> pressed downward . . . There would be holocausts of fire in the
> woods . . . The brutality of the land somehow evoked joy in
> Karen.

Now she takes her father's arm as they leave the church. When she opens the
door, "the swirling snow . . . turned white and cold and innocent, like the
disorder of her brain." Only in the implications of Karen's changed perceptions of the weather (the savage extremities that had once lured her are now
harmless) and in her determination to retain clarity of mind can we make even
a tenuous judgment of the degree to which her individuation will be consol-
idated and retained. She turns lovingly to the now feeble patriarch who would
have taught her to murder. She agrees to re-enter the life of the family and
to participate in the ritual of the church, but to guard her self-created state.
She seems to know not only that there is no fate that cannot be surmounted
by scorn, but also that—if *she* chooses—there is no fate that cannot be borne
with patience, endurance and love. Her knowledge has been dearly bought:
Karen is a misfit and an alien, victim of her own stubborn integrity as surely
as Shar has become the ultimate victim of his.

Jung points out that the task of creating a self can be accomplished only
by the resolution of the conflict between the conscious and the unconscious
through experience, never by understanding alone. The integration of the
unconscious in which we observe Karen Herz tends to induce panic in
civilized people because of its relation to insanity—a fact of which Karen is
keenly aware when she concludes that it is insane to look for meaning in
existence and insane not to.

Further, the traditional and conservative spirit of society which is in-
imical to the acceptance of the unconscious still wears the earthly garment
of the church and the father—most obdurately so in a rural and orthodox
area such as Oates's Eden County. Therefore, in acknowledging the reality
of the unconscious, that awakening force which moves her out of Eden
County, and in attempting to make that darker side of the self which Jung
calls the shadow, a co-determining ethical factor in her life, Karen offends
against the spirit of convention which for centuries has regulated the psychic
life of the individual by means of the church and the family—the institutions
against which she revolts.

Speaking of the inadequacy of what is legally, morally and socially
approved to encourage—or even permit—the creation of a tenable sense of
self, Jung says:

> Man's great task is the adaptation of himself to reality and the
> recognition of himself as an instrument for the expression of life

according to his individual possibilities. It is in his privilege as self-creator that his highest purpose is found.

and:

The bringing together of the conscious and the unconscious is a task facing not only individuals, but whole civilizations. The political and social isms of our day preach every conceivable kind of ideal, but, under this mask, they pursue the goal of inhibiting the possibilities of individual development . . . This problem cannot be solved collectively, because the masses are not changed unless the individual changes . . . The bettering of a general ill begins with the individual, and then only when he makes himself and not others responsible.

In *With Shuddering Fall* Oates has created a complex paradigm of the tension which exists between the entelechy of personal individuation and the societal forces resistant to it.

JOHN GARDNER

The Strange Real World

Bellefleur is the most ambitious book to come so far from that alarming phenomenon Joyce Carol Oates. However one may carp, the novel is proof, if any seems needed, that she is one of the great writers of our time. *Bellefleur* is a symbolic summation of all this novelist has been doing for twenty-some years, a magnificent piece of daring, a tour de force of imagination and intellect.

In *Bellefleur* Miss Oates makes a heroic attempt to transmute the almost inherently goofy tradition of the gothic (ghosts, shape-shifters, vampires and all that) into serious art. If any writer can bring it off (some will claim it's already been done), Joyce Carol Oates seems the writer to do it. One thinks of the astonishing, utterly convincing scene in her novel *The Assassins* where Stephen Petrie, a child sitting at his desk in school, has his terrifying out-of-the-body experience, and the scenes in which Hugh, his artist brother, has his brushes with the Angel of Death; one thinks of the psychic business in *Childwold,* the ominous rappings of tyrannical spirit in *Wonderland,* the horror-ridden, love-redeemed world of William James and his circle in *Night-Side;* above all one thinks of *Son of the Morning,* Miss Oates's magnificently convincing study of a snake-handler and miracle-worker, Nathan Vickery.

What we learn, reading *Bellefleur,* is that Joyce Carol Oates is essentially a realist. She can write persuasively of out-of-the-body experiences because she believes in them. But she does not really believe in a brutal

From *The New York Times Book Review* (20 July 1980). © 1980 by the New York Times Co., Inc.

half-wit boy who can turn into a dog, a man who is really a bear, vampires or mountain gnomes. (In one scene members of the Bellefleur family come across some gnomes escaped from Washington Irving, thunderously bowling on a mountain meadow. One of the gnomes gets captured and, though his whole race is inexplicably mean, turns into a devoted servant of the novel's heroine, Leah. Why? Who knows? The world is mysterious.)

Miss Oates believes in these legendary characters only as symbols and the problem is that they are not symbols of the same class as those she has been using for years, the symbols provided by the world as it is when it is viewed (as Miss Oates always views it) as a Christian Platonist's "vast array of emblems." The only really frightening scenes in *Bellefleur* deal with real-world atrocities—a boy's stoning of another boy, for instance, or the murder of a family by a bunch of drunken thugs—and these scenes in fact come nowhere near the horror of scenes in earlier novels by Miss Oates, such as the murder of Yvonne in *The Assassins*. What drives Miss Oates's fiction is her phobias: that is, her fear that normal life may suddenly turn monstrous. Abandoning verisimilitude for a different mode (the willing suspension of disbelief), she loses her ability to startle us with sudden nightmare. Still the tale is sometimes thrilling. The opening chapter (strongly recalling that wonderful collection of ghost stories, *Night-Side*) has prowling spirits, a weird storm, a glorious scary castle in the Adirondacks, all presented in an absolutely masterly, chilling style; but the chapter's crowning moment comes when a frightening, vicious, rat-like thing, which none of the frightened occupants can identify, is allowed out of the rain (screaming) into the house and, when seen in the morning, turns out to be a mysteriously beautiful cat. The transformation startles us, catches us completely by surprise (classic Oates), fills us with awe and vague dread, prompting the question we so often ask when reading her: *What in heaven's name is the universe up to now?*

I cannot summarize the plot of *Bellefleur;* for one thing, it's too complex—an awesome construction, in itself a work of genius—and for another, plot surprises are part of the novel's glory. Suffice it to say that this is the saga of the weird, sometimes immensely rich Bellefleur family over several generations, a story focused mainly on Gideon Bellefleur and his power-mad, somewhat psychic, very beautiful wife Leah, their three children (one of them extremely psychic) and the servants and relatives, living and dead, who inhabit the castle and its environs. It's a story of the world's changeableness, of time and eternity, space and soul, pride and physicality versus love.

Much as one admires the ambition of *Bellefleur,* the novel is slightly

marred by it: It too noticeably labors after greatness. The book has most of
the familiar Oates weaknesses: the panting, melodramatic style she too
often allows herself; the heavy, heavy symbolism; and occasional esthetic
miscalculations that perhaps come from thinking too subtly, forgetting that
first of all a story must be a completely persuasive lie. In *Bellefleur*, the
artifice undermines emotional power, makes the book cartoonish.

I will give just one example to show what I mean. At the end of
Bellefleur, Gideon, the focal character—now so wasted that people call him
"Old Skin and Bones"—crashes his plane and destroys himself and his
family estate. He does this in company with a personage known only as "the
Rasche woman." We have no idea why she willingly goes along, knowing
his intent—a hard thing to believe. Miss Oates, who can create a totally
convincing character in half a page, makes a point of not characterizing the
Rasche woman at all; no one, not even her lover Gideon, knows her first
name. I think Miss Oates expects her most devoted readers to know that the
name has appeared before (for instance, in *The Assassins* there is a Marxist
called Rasche, or sometimes Raschke, an equally shadowy figure). As
Melville once said, "Something further may follow of this Masquerade." It's
an interesting business, another reminder that sometimes the fabric of reality rips and strange beings crawl through; but a catastrophe scene at the
end of a novel is a bad place to sacrifice convincingness for the sake of larger
meaning.

I have mentioned already that the novel's construction is complex. I
must add that the construction sometimes forces the author into what will
seem to some readers unfortunate corners. In the first few chapters Miss
Oates mentions numerous small details (various queer artifacts, including a
drum made of human skin and numerous odd characters, such as an aunt
who never comes out by daylight, a mad, saintly hermit and so on). Each of
these details will later get its fully developed story, and some of the details
set up in the beginning will lead to stories (motifs) to which the novel will
return repeatedly. Unhappily, some of these motifs or plot strands—whose
recurrence is unavoidable once the machinery gets rolling—are somewhat
boring. For example there is the child Raphael, whose chief—in fact only—
interest in life is, well, this stupid pond. He stares into it, every few chapters,
and sees there a framed sample of teeming, ever-changing total reality. (Miss
Oates's descriptions of nature in *Bellefleur* are astonishingly good, but after
a while a pond is a pond is a pond.) Or again, there is Jedediah Bellefleur,
one of the recurring types in Miss Oates's fiction, the saintly man who, like
Stephen in *The Assassins* or Nathan in *Son of the Morning* loses his hold on
God.

Jedediah is interesting, up to a point, and he's both dramatically and symbolically crucial to the story; but I at least am sorry when, every few chapters, we have to return to Jedediah and watch him staring at something improbably called Mount Blanc or struggling with his not very interesting demons. ("He's nuts, that's all," we say, and slog on.) In the end Jedediah proves worth it all. He loses his sense of holy mission, thus becoming an appropriate focus of the blind and raging life force Miss Oates writes about in all her work. Jedediah cares nothing about the world, nothing about God, but after his family's near-extinction by massacre, he is persuaded to leave his mountain and found the new Bellefleur line. The point is, of course, one made in *Son of the Morning* and elsewhere. Loving God completely, one cares nothing about the world, not even about people, whom one sees, rightly, as mere instances; but on the other hand, completely loving oneself or the world, one loses one's soul and becomes (as does Gideon in the end) a figure of death.

Whatever its faults, *Bellefleur* is simply brilliant. What do we ask of a book except that it be wonderful to read? An interesting story with profound implications? The whole religious-philosophical view of Joyce Carol Oates is here cleanly and dramatically stated. She has been saying for years, in book after book (stories, poems, a play and literary criticism) that the world is Platonic. We are the expression of one life force, but once individuated we no longer know it, so that we recoil in horror from the expression of the same force in other living beings. "Don't *touch* me," Gideon Bellefleur keeps saying, as Yvonne Petrie said in *The Assassins*, Laney said in *Childwold* and a host of other characters said elsewhere. Blinded to our oneness, we all become assassins, vampires, ghosts. We are all unreflectable nonimages in mirrors, creatures of time, and time is an illusion; we are all sexual maniacs, lovers engaged in a violent struggle to become totally one with those we love (copulation and murder are all but indistinguishable); we are all crazily in love with the past—first our own Edenic childhood, second the whole past of the world. So Leah, in *Bellefleur*, strives to reconquer the whole immense original Bellefleur estate—and ends up dead, not even buried, burnt up with the house after the plane crash.

Bellefleur is a medieval allegory of *caritas versus cupiditas*, love and selflessness versus pride and selfishness. The central symbol of the novel is change, baffling complexity, mystery. One character makes "crazy quilts" in which only she can see the pattern. Another has been trying all his life to map the Bellefleur holdings, but everything keeps changing—rivers change their courses, mountains shrink. Time is crazy. In fact what is known in Shakespeare criticism as "sliding time" becomes a calculated madness in

Bellefleur. Chapters leap backward and forward through the years—and that's the least of it. Our main dramatic focus, though she's a minor character, is the psychic child Germaine Bellefleur, whom we follow from birth to the age of four. But *in the same time* her father passes through twenty or thirty years; and the setting passes through something like a thousand years, with hints of a time-span even greater. People regularly get taller or shorter, depending on . . . whatever. The holy mountain in the Adirondacks to which Jedediah goes to find God is at first 10,000 feet high but by the end of the novel only 3,000 feet high.

Joyce Carol Oates has always been, for those who look closely, a religious novelist, but this is the most openly religious of her books—not that she argues any one sectarian point of view. Here as in several of her earlier works the Angel of Death is an important figure, but here for the first time the Angel of Life (not simply resignation) is the winner. In the novel's final chapters Gideon Bellefleur turns his back on all he has been since birth, a sensualist; starves himself until we see him as a death figure; finally becomes his family's Angel of Death.

But there's one further chapter, set far in the past, entitled "The Angel." Whereas Gideon's flight and kamikaze self-destruction as he crashes his plane into his ancestral home are presented in mystical metaphors (the rise into spiritual air, and so on), the final chapter is utterly physical. An Indian boy, a friend of the family, comes to Jedediah on his mountain and tells him to return to the world. With no belief in God and no interest in the worldly, Jedediah returns to the woman he once loved and becomes the father of those who will figure in this novel, becomes the instrument of the blind life force that, accidentally, indifferently, makes everything of value, makes everything beautiful by the simple virtue of its momentary existence. Thanks to Jedediah, God goes on senselessly humming, discovering Himself. That is, in Miss Oates's vision, the reason we have to live and the reason life, however dangerous, can be a joy, once we understand our situation: We are God's body.

Joyce Carol Oates is a "popular" novelist because her stories are suspenseful (and the suspense is never fake: The horror will really come, as well as, sometimes, the triumph), because her sex scenes are steamy and because when she describes a place you think you're there. Pseudo-intellectuals seem to hate that popularity and complain, besides, that she "writes too much." (For pseudo-intellectuals there are always too many books.) To real intellectuals Miss Oates's work tends to be appealing, partly because her vision is huge, well-informed and sound, and partly because they too like suspense, brilliant descriptions and sex. Though *Bellefleur* is not her best book, in my opinion it's a wonderful book all the same. By one two-page thunderstorm she makes the rest of us novelists wonder why we left the farm. How strange the play of light and shadow in her graveyards! How splendid the Bellefleurs' decaying mansion! How convincing and individual the characters are—and so many of them! In one psychic moment, when the not-yet-two-year-old Germaine cries "Bird—bird—bird!" and points at the window a moment before a bird crashes into it, breaking its neck, we're forced to ask again how anyone can possibly write such books, such absolutely convincing scenes, rousing in us, again and again, the familiar Oates effect, the point of all her art: joyful terror gradually ebbing toward wonder.

THOMAS R. EDWARDS

The House of Atreus Now

With twelve novels and eleven books of stories published within the past two decades, Joyce Carol Oates must be our most productive writer of serious fiction. Like such other big producers as Doris Lessing, John Updike and Norman Mailer, she recalls an old-fashioned idea of the novelist as one who does not occasionally unveil a carefully chiseled "work of art" but who conducts a continuous and risky exercise of the imagination through the act of writing. Where a new novel by John Barth, Saul Bellow, Joseph Heller or Thomas Pynchon is deemed, whatever its merit, a literary event, a new novel by Joyce Carol Oates is, we may feel, another new novel by Oates, better or worse than the last one, certainly different from it, but hard to see as a major demand upon our attention. This immediate response is unfair but perhaps not lasting. With occasional exceptions (Joyce, Flaubert), we finally care most about novelists like Dickens, George Eliot, Balzac, Tolstoy, Hardy, James, Conrad, Lawrence or Faulkner whose work is copious enough to constitute a "world," and though no guarantees can be offered, energy like Joyce Carol Oates's may find an eventual reward.

Her newest book, *Angel of Light,* is a political novel, though one less interested in the practice of politics itself than in its power to evoke certain deep human impulses toward violence. The story is very generally based on the fall of the House of Atreus; once again a brother and sister seek to avenge the killing of their father by murdering their mother and her lover. But here the myth is updated, and altered, by the terms in which power is

From *The New York Times Book Review* (16 August 1981). © 1981 by the New York Times Co.

now exercised in America—the shadowy intersections of government, business, finance, ideology and organized crime.

Maurice J. Halleck, a rich, idealistic public servant, director of the Commission for the Ministry of Justice, is in the late seventies suspected of having taken a bribe to quash an investigation into a major corporation's illegal political interventions in South America. Halleck resigns, separates from his society-hostess wife, takes to drink, and finally, in June 1979, commits suicide, leaving behind a confession of his guilt in the bribery scandal. His daughter Kirsten, a disturbed, anorexic, drug-dependent boarding-school girl, is sure that her father was innocent. Without hard evidence, she just *knows* that his confession was forged and that he was murdered by his wife, Isabel, and the ambitious Nick Martens, his friend since school days, his assistant and then his successor as director, and by general belief Isabel's lover for many years. Kirsten persuades her brother Owen, a smug, success-oriented senior at Princeton who is bound for Harvard Law and a career like his father's, that her terrible, improbable imaginings are true, and together they plot to serve justice by killing Isabel and Nick.

Miss Oates gives this grim story an epigraph from Bernard Mandeville, the eighteenth-century master of a moral "realism" cunningly designed to be both heartening and profoundly demoralizing: "What we call Evil in this World, Moral as well as Natural, is the grand Principle that makes us sociable Creatures, the solid Basis, the Life and Support of all Trades and Employments without Exception: That there we must look for the true Original of all Arts and Sciences, and that the Moment Evil ceases, the Society must be spoiled if not totally dissolved." But if the *Angel of Light* is a philosophical novel about the impossibility of justice in a fallen, irredeemably compromised human community, the book (in a good nineteenth-century way) accommodates other kinds of interest too—it is at once a kind of thriller, a romance of desire and betrayal in high society, a psychological examination of alienated youth, a study of marital failure in a declining aristocracy, an uncovering of the personal roots of public violence.

The narrative relies on temporal crosscutting, between the six months in 1980 during which the children conceive and pursue their plot of revenge and flashbacks of Maurice Halleck's life as it is woven into the lives of Nick, Isabel and his children. It all began in 1947, on a white-water river in Canada, when Halleck, a rather inept and unprepossessing rich kid with deep religious yearnings, was saved from drowning by Nick, his capable, attractive, fiercely competitive prep-school friend, a scholarship boy whose

future is assured by the gratitude of Maurie and his family. This first bond-
ing is complicated by Nick's later testings of Maurie's devotion. In 1955,
when Maurie first introduces Nick to his provocative fiancée, Isabel, the two
disappear together for a suspiciously long walk on the beach; in 1967,
watched by a fuming Isabel who has a party to give, Nick and Maurie play
an interminable tennis match, protracted because Nick, who is normally
much the better player, is determined to win the last game but somehow
can't; just before his death in 1979, Maurie struggles to understand and
accept what his final talks with Isabel and Nick have revealed, that he has
been less central to their lives than he realized. And while this history
approaches the catastrophic present, the Halleck children—Orestes and
Electra in Washington—pursue their bloody design without knowing clearly
how the past has created, and betrayed, the present.

I'm not sure that Miss Oates adds a great deal to what writers like
Louis Auchincloss, Frederick Buechner, John Cheever and John Knowles
have told us about the moral life in our old ruling class. Even at their most
vivid moments—as when the aggressive Nick confesses a secret yearning to
be not himself but just "a person," without family, history or intentions—
Miss Oates's adults may owe as much to other fiction as to fresh observation or imagining. But the story centers on Owen and Kirsten, and their
search through violence for an exactitude of justice that, as Mandeville
suggested, no human society could survive. In her portrayal of the Halleck
children, Miss Oates achieves a fresh and frightening picture of a desire that
exceeds any available attainment. Owen and Kirsten, whom Miss Oates
makes descendants of John Brown of Osawatomie, strive to reconstruct
reality in the image of their dream of justice, as their ancestor had once also
tried to do, with equally shattering effect.

Thoreau provided the title for this novel when he called John Brown
"an Angel of Light," and we may safely presume that, like Joyce Carol
Oates, Thoreau was cognizant of who the first angel of light was and what
befell him. One of that Lucifer's stoutest champions, William Blake, in fact
presides over Owen and Kirsten's great enterprise; they debate, with touching uncertainty, the meaning of various of Blake's "Proverbs of Hell" before
finding one whose significance unarguably suits their purpose: "What is
now proved was once only imagined." For them this suggests that destructive action can confirm and justify their conviction that their father was
framed and killed by a wife and friend who served not only their own paltry
desires but also served (somehow) a conspiracy of the power structure,
whose identification of realpolitik with reality was threatened by Maurice
Halleck's almost saintly probity.

We are for a while free to regard the children's imaginings as being just what they sound like, a fantasy born of grief and precarious stability. Kirsten was a wild, self-destructive girl long before her father's fall, and in the pompous, buttoned-down conformity of boys like Owen there often does lurk a repressed other self nearing critical mass. And, of course, public events in the children's formative years engendered paranoid delusions in older and sounder minds than theirs. Since suspense is one of the book's pleasures, I must not say too much here; but it does start to appear that the children's imaginings may not be as utterly fantastic as they seem. There are real questions about Halleck's guilt, about Isabel's virtue and Nick's loyalty, even about how remote this personal tragedy is from political and corporate maleficence. If what begins to be proved is not exactly what once was only imagined by Owen and Kirsten, in a social world regulated by Evil, some uncomfortable possibilities do suggest themselves. In such a world exact proof is hard to come by—one seemingly knowledgeable source says that Nick was a CIA agent, while another claims that he was an undercover Communist, and he may have been neither, or both—but such indeterminacy itself hints at moral horror. On the other hand, those who would dissolve ambiguity into single vision by an act of moral will point toward an alternative and commensurate horror—here exemplified by the American Silver Doves Revolutionary Army, a group of underemployed ex-graduate students turned Maoist terrorists who convert Owen's personal quest for justice into service in their own violent cause.

Having recently seen so good a novelist as Mary McCarthy turn somewhat similar material into a talky, unconvincing ideological puppet show in *Cannibals and Missionaries*," I'm much impressed by Miss Oates's ability to enter and explore the personal sources of the high-minded violence that's now such a familiar fact of public life. I'm impressed too by how clearly she remembers that her first duty is not to judge but to understand. Judgment of a kind is suggested, particularly in the novel's epilogue, where a survivor of this children's crusade, living alone and unoccupied on the coast of Maine, ponders "the emptiness and beauty of a world uncontaminated by, and unguided by, human volition"; but if the choice of solitude and a resigned acceptance of the world as a mystery whose secret is not to be discovered constitutes a form of judgment, it is not one that offers ready comfort.

Angel of Light may be another chapter in Joyce Carol Oates's ongoing exercise of the imagination, but it is also a strong and fascinating novel on its own terms. Coming after her haunting fantasy *Bellefleur,* which in effect levitates above the history and geography of the known world to report that its larger moral contours remain deeply mysterious, *Angel of Light* gravitates back toward the terra firma of a novel like Miss Oates's *them,* where social circumstance and personal fate are closely and realistically linked. But enough mystery persists in *Angel of Light* to suggest that this prolific and various novelist is staking out new fictional ground.

FREDERICK R. KARL

Modes of Survival

Sections of *them* devoted to Loretta, the mother of the main character, Maureen, seem to derive directly from Dreiser, an updating of Jennie Gerhardt, or reminiscent of Sister Carrie. Loretta's life appears caught by all the familiar elements of doom—poor neighborhood, petty crime of the young men around her, hopelessness of young women growing up resigned to their roles, "protective" older brother, who serves as a father surrogate, sudden crime (here a murder), marriage to a young man (Howard Wendall) who slowly descends into impotence. These elements serve as traps, and they are cyclical: what begins when Loretta is sixteen will recur when she is twenty-six, and after. Children appear regularly to ensure she can never escape. Thus, Loretta seems a person who will pass on to her children those same qualities of entrapment.

But like Dreiser's Carrie, although in a different style, Loretta is a survivor; and Oates's entire presentation is a tableau of survivors: how women, in effect, survive their men. In every way, the men are deadly creatures, and they dominate the lives of their women. But they do not triumph. The men are violent—for example, Loretta's second husband, Pat Furlong (a horse of a man), severely beats up Maureen and terrorizes the household. He is a successor to Loretta's own brother, Brock, who shoots Bernie Malin dead when he finds Bernie in bed with Loretta. Loretta's father controls his household by way of bouts of insanity and drinking; her first husband, Howard, sets the pace of the house by way of negative qualities:

From *American Fictions 1940/1980.* © 1983 by Frederick R. Karl. Harper & Row, 1983.

sullenness, potential violence, alcoholism. At nearly every stage, the men seem in control—either physically or by way of negative force; but the women survive them. Loretta marries to get away from her brother; Howard is killed in an accident; Furlong goes to prison; Maureen seduces a college professor in order to reestablish her life.

Modes of survival differ, of course. Loretta surrounds herself with similar women, proves tougher and cagier than her men, provides them with just sufficient services to control them. Young Maureen uses school and then the library as a way "out," as moments of peace, although the school situation is destroyed for her when she loses the secretary's book of minutes. But the library remains a sanctuary. Jane Austen, among others, introduces her to alternative worlds where she can, temporarily, escape—and escape she will, even after the severe beating Furlong administers. Her means of escape is through prostitution, and Oates's handling of these scenes is expert.

As the novel shifts toward her, Maureen has felt herself emptied out. She has nothing but contempt for her situation, but mainly for Furlong, whose heavy, smelly, hairy presence is a desecration even of their minimal home. Her brother Jules had felt that way about their father, now she about her stepfather. "There was nothing in her but a hatred for him so diffuse that it was like her own blood, coursing mechanically through her. She ransacked her mind but there was nothing in it. Everything was emptied out, exhausted. She might have been inhabiting her mother's body." Even books can no longer stir her.

The image of emptiness is, by way of contrasts, a cogent one in postwar fiction. Not the emptiness of Hemingway's characters, who raise the quality almost to heroic terms, that in postwar fiction is sheer blankness, in contrast with rich life around: a negative element which works by opposites as well as by definition of an individual. It is not a condition that can be filled by the elements of life; nothing will sustain that emptiness. It is not even Kafkaesque, which has some morbidly comic dimension to it. It is close to anomie, to utter silence. It is outside space and time, in some dimension that lies in the sub- or unconscious, and it is completely countercultural. It cannot be reached by the culture, although on occasion that can be tapped by the individual. Maureen has to learn how to deal with emptiness; and her success or failure is, for Oates, a paradigm of what women must do—that emptiness, for her, defines in the main where women are. Loretta sinks into it; Maureen still has options, however circumscribed.

In the circumstances, Maureen feels something snap, which means she can control her emotional life, and she can use the one thing she has to make

money: her young body. The man she sells herself to offers kindness, interest, and money, which she saves in a book of poetry—a practice that leads
to her undoing, when Furlong discovers her cache and beats her. In describing Maureen's physical reaction to a man's body, Oates is superb: "His skin
was a man's skin, a little rough. It felt almost sandy beneath her fingers. He
himself was a little rough, and so she seemed to be guiding him with her
hands on his back and her mouth near his. A man was like a machine: one
of those machines at the laundromat where she dragged the laundry. There
were certain cycles to go through."

By turning sexual intercourse into a laundry cycle, Maureen has discovered her way out: mechanizing feeling, she controls it, whereas the man
will always be humbled by it. She has learned what Loretta also found, that
men can be manipulated despite their physical power and their desire for
domination.

For the sake of the novel's forward movement in real time and space,
Oates has chosen to introduce the actual "Maureen Wendall." "This is a
work of history in fictional form," she writes, "that is, in personal perspective, which is the only kind of history that exists." Maureen was a student
in Oates's class at the University of Detroit, whose life seemed to be so
absorbing—and, incidentally, internally similar enough to Oates's own to
create interest—that the novelist felt: "This is the only kind of fiction that
is real." The novel about Maureen became *them:* "Them" would heroize or
memorialize; Maureen must ascend from a lowercase "them."

Two-thirds through the novel, Oates interrupts with two letters from
Maureen. The technique serves primarily as the letter did in the Victorian
novel, functioning for purposes of plot—like Tess's letter to Angel Clare in
the Hardy novel—and giving the novelist another means of conveying narrative dimensions, however unwieldy. It is a deliberate way of introducing
a naturalistic element—the cause and effect of the real world—while insisting on the prerogatives of the fictional world. It offers a good deal to the
development of the nonfiction novel.

Maureen's two letters come in 1966, nine years after she has emerged
from a near-comatose state, her depression after Furlong's beating so great
she has grown enormously fat, pimply, unresponsive to stimuli. She has, in
her withdrawal, become infantile, and her mother can handle her only by
hand-feeding her and letting her settle into a childlike existence. What
awakens her is the sudden appearance of Loretta's brother Brock, the man
who had shot Bernie in bed. Brock is a terrible failure, but he encourages
Maureen; and a letter from her brother Jules supports her further. Parts of
her body begin to cohere; she feels connected, like a machine reassembled.

In the nine years since her awakening, as she tells Oates, she has taken some control of her life. She has moved into a single room of her own, taken a position in an office, and started to pursue a degree at the university, where Oates had her as a student, and failed her. At twenty-six, she writes to tell Oates she failed her in the course, failed her out of the university, and in turn, failed *her*.

The letter is a remarkable document, for it suggests that Oates, while brilliant in the classroom, missed altogether what Maureen was—the student had asked for a dimension the teacher could not give, not as a woman, not as a person. "One year I lay in bed in silence and a few years later I was writing papers for you, trying to write. You failed me. You flunked me out of school." She says she does not condemn; she does not even judge. Oates gave her an "F" for "Lack of coherence and development."

What makes the letter so remarkable is the way it uses a "marking system," a classroom procedure which puts walls between people in the system (Oates) and those who must find their way outside it (Maureen). It is not simply well-to-do versus poor, or have versus have-not, or educated versus uneducated; it goes to the heart of democratic procedure, which in its egalitarianism is ruthless, uncaring, cold-blooded. This is essentially what Maureen accuses Oates of being: of existing so cocooned (her writing, her sense of "art from life," her husband driving her to the campus, her shielding herself from all intrusions) that she becomes impervious to touch.

Maureen says she has lived off hate of her former teacher, and we must not forget that Oates has chosen to include this damaging letter, her version of what Maureen wrote. "But yes. I hate you and no one else, not even those men, not even Furlong. I hate you and that is the only certain thing in me. Not love for the man I want to marry [her evening teacher at her next school] but hate for you. Hate for you, with your books and words and your knowing so much that never happened, in a perfect form, you being driven to school by your husband, and now there are even photographs of you in the paper sometimes, you with your knowledge while I've lived a lifetime already and turned myself inside and out and got nothing out of it, not a thing. . . . I lived my life but there is no form to it. No shape."

Everything Oates had taught about forms, shapes, and systems is questioned by the reality of a countering life, by the history of a single person. This is, as I have already suggested, a common theme in postwar fiction, reflecting as it does the American hatred of the very goods and materials supporting the culture. Bellow's Herzog in his Vermont farmhouse dreams of a simpler existence, despising the complications of the larger system, all the while drawing on services from that culture. Oates demonstrates

Maureen's intense hatred of Oates's world, and yet her survival depends on her acquiring a piece of that world: a husband (any decent man!), her own house, a child, curtains on the windows, a settled and stable existence outside her Wendall background. She cannot speak of art forming life, because life has had no shape for her.

Oates's insight is so grand because it folds both sexes into a system-antisystem confrontation while showing how the conflict more directly affects the woman. Maureen's struggle is, I feel, the key "woman's life" since the Second World War, not only for its qualities of survival, but for thrusting into relief Oates's own very different, and very sheltered, existence. They were seemingly very alike, Oates says; and yet her intelligence and talent put her in a category of escape: through achievement in school, then through achievement with her fiction. Yet they were similar in their awareness of women trapped, forced to escape by bizarre means. Maureen's life, then, becomes prototypical because it is played off against Oates's, because of that one long letter which, while describing her, reflects the other.

One wonders how Herzog would have looked if Bellow had provided an external version of him: Herzog observed through others' eyes, not simply through his own perceptions of himself. A male writer does not consider such self-criticism appropriate. Since Bellow's acceptance of Herzog's self-indulgence does not permit this, the latter is given his own reins, drives his own team, and no one, except himself, judges. Similarly, we wonder how Mailer's American Dreamer, Rojack, would have looked from the outside, although Mailer's obsession with himself could not countenance this. Rojack remains in his own class or category, a fighter winning against his own shadow, not against an opponent.

A parallel movement to Maureen in *them* involves her brother Jules, and here we have a structural element that calls into question Oates's method. Jules is the footloose opposite of Maureen: as obsessively as she demands some stability for herself, he rejects it, becoming the archetypical American male, seeking spatial adventures and losing mightily in the exchange with America. At every turn, Jules is defeated by the country, its people, its size, its values. He is, however, a survivor; and even his love for the rich-born Nadine, who shoots him in the chest, does not doom him. He survives the wound, survives his obsession with Nadine, survives anarchic elements in himself. He apparently thrives on acting out the wildness that constituted his background.

Jules and Maureen are sides of Dreiser's Clyde Griffiths. They identify with his upward mobility, and they contain within themselves unidentifiable elements of doom. Jules branches off to become one type of Clyde, surely in his relationship to Nadine, whereas Maureen finally rejects that aspect of herself. The hand of Dreiser lies heavily over *them* in that stress on ordinary detail which becomes, with art, the generality of the human condition. Oates is almost singular among contemporary novelists in being able to evoke the Dreiserian social sense without sinking into programmatic naturalism.

Jules represents Oates's opportunity to get beyond herself, to relocate the Maureen in her, and to explore a double or twin. Although Jules is older and independent almost from childhood, he is devoted to Maureen and, in his way, attached to the family; he sends money, he writes, he never fully deserts his mother or sister. While the other siblings fade into the background, Jules remains in Maureen's consciousness: as possibility, potentiality, ideas of escape. Still, Jules is caught by his own form of doom, in the person of Nadine, who comes from Grosse Pointe, is obviously wealthy, and yet is herself foundering in some doom-filled sensibility. She and Jules run off, and he helps to support her by way of a series of petty crimes; then when he falls ill, she abandons him, unable to deal with giving. As a vampire, she does not lack victims.

The Jules-Nadine relationship, although a dimension Oates felt was necessary, lacks center. It is full of frenzy, wild passion; but ultimately cold. Oates is not very effective in her scenes of erotic passion, imposed on us by a skillful writer who is outside her metier.

Oates is superb, however, with Maureen, focused, pitched, passionately sympathetic with Maureen's desire for identity and existence. This is one of the strongest presentations of character in postwar fiction not solely a woman writing about a woman, but an author writing about a character. She has the same intensity here that James Jones had with Prewitt and, especially, Warden; Oates as a writer recalls Jones: his honesty, his intensity, his centering himself in Dreiserian forms, and yet his recognition that he must break out into something less binding.

Unfortunately, Jules and Nadine become dead-end characters. That is, they heave and strain against each other or against their personal demons, but remain only possibility. Similarly, Oates's attempt at achieving a vision of Detroit—the typifying American city of the late sixties—is not fully successful. As background for the Wendalls, once they move from the grandmother's farm, Detroit is always present: a discontinuous mix of whites and blacks living in fear and hatred of each other, white bigotry matched by black violence. This part Oates catches well: that sense of people in poor circumstances forced to live near each other and forming "tribes" or primal hordes as ways of excluding outsiders. Black imagination, white hatred, fear on both sides, a rising crime rate, unsafe streets, casual violence, all characterize the Wendalls' world as Maureen grows up. Late in the novel, with Jules on the margins, she focuses upon a group of revolutionaries, led by Dr. Mort Piercy, a rich and successful young man who preaches revolution. The scene is an effort at sixties explosion, urban apocalypse, a sense of final things. Yet it appears tacked on; at least the riot does, although it existed in fact.

What partially vitiates the power of Maureen's tale is the aborted quality of other elements: Jules in nearly all his activities, although his presence does seem necessary for analogy, contrast, textual thickness; the finale with Detroit apocalypse, and the emergence of Jules as a figure of power; the linkage to constant violence, focus on guns, their use and presence; the subsidiary characters, who appear and then usually vanish without defining themselves. The line of strength in the novel lies with mother-daughter; then with Maureen's resolve to undermine her evening teacher's marriage. Oates does not show that plan in sufficient detail, only the resolve, even foreshortening the meeting with the teacher's wife. That showdown, in which one woman survives by undermining another, is told in retrospect, Maureen to Loretta, after the fact. Yet the process of undermining, of subverting another, innocent woman's marriage, has potential interest, for Randolph's wife is as much a victim as is Maureen. Yet Oates was interested, apparently, in larger dimensions, and she dissipated the immense power of the primary line of development. Nevertheless, whatever deterrents we discover, *them* is a fitting capstone to the sixties: not only for women's issues, or for the sense of urban violence, or for the renewal of social and class values in American fiction; not only for these reasons, but for Oates's intense fidelity to a vision of life.

SAMUEL CHASE COALE

Joyce Carol Oates:
Contending Spirits

Joyce Carol Oates's Manichean vision of contemporary America threatens
to overwhelm any literary form she uses to try to encompass it. Emotions
override reason; monologue buries meaning; individual characters dissolve
beneath the full force of their feelings, insights, and omnivorous yearnings.
Even her apparent method of creation suggests the power these characters
and emotional forces have upon her: "When I'm with people I often fall into
a kind of waking sleep, a day-dreaming about the people, the strangers, who
are to be the 'characters' in the story or novel I will be writing. . . . At times
my head seems crowded; there is a kind of pressure inside it, almost a
frightening physical sense of confusion, fullness, dizziness. . . . 'My characters' really dictate themselves to me. I am not free of them, really. . . . They
have the autonomy of characters in a dream." It is as if exorcism replaces
fiction. Confession overpowers its literary container.

   Dark dualistic design stalks Oates's haunted mind as starkly as it did
Hawthorne's, but with more sheer emotional power and force: "In the
novels I have written, I have tried to give a shape to certain obsessions of
mid-century Americans—a confusion of love and money, of the categories
of public and private experience, of demonic urge I sense all around me, an
urge to violence as the answer to all problems, an urge to self-annihilation,
suicide, the ultimate experience and the ultimate surrender." Dualism becomes a dominant demonic force that, if outrun, suggests both an ultimate
freedom and ultimate self-destruction. As G. F. Waller suggests, Oates tears

From *In Hawthorne's Shadow: American Romance from Melville to Mailer.* © 1985
by The University Press of Kentucky.

through that very American sensibility with its often uneasy alliance between the mystical and the material, "the dislocation between dream and
materialism in America." In fact, "to assert the primacy of the unquantifiable
seems necessarily to end in the Manicheism which has constantly characterized American experience." "All the books published under my name in
the past ten years," Oates asserts, "have been formalized, complex propo-
sitions about the nature of personality and its relationship to a specific
culture (contemporary America)." Obsessed with the Western myth of the
self, the ego, Oates presses that fiction to its limits, seeking necessarily some
wider space beyond, some other ultimate reality beyond the materialized,
self-conscious self in contemporary America.

Violence alone seems capable of breaking through the boundaries of
the Western ego. Only a palpable, forceful wrenching can shatter such
historical self-images. "Violence is always an affirmation," Oates insists,
and in her remarks on Dostoyevski she seems to reveal her own method for
writing fiction: "It seems likely that the acts of violence—the sheer consummation of murderous impulses designed to 'change one's life'—are the bases
upon which the novels are written; the ideological dialogues come second."
Oates sounds similar to the more traditionally Catholic O'Connor in her
insistence on the primacy of violence to break through outmoded habits,
stale rites of Western consciousness. In fact, in writing about O'Connor she
insists that one "can be delivered from the trance of self only by violence."
Passion alone can liberate and save, no matter how it is expressed, how it
erupts through and within social experience. "What are we except passion,"
Oates states, "and how are we to survive when this passion breaks its dikes
and flows out into nature?" How, indeed! And yet without the overflow of
passion, there is nothing: "Nihilism is overcome by the breaking-down of
the dikes between human beings, the flowing forth of passion." A very thin
line, then, between liberation and destruction, creation and collapse.

The self battles an incomprehensible world, whether etched in numbing
poverty—an experience from Oates's own family background—or steeped
in the sheer pervasiveness of American welath and material goods. And it
needs that incomprehensible world to battle against. Oates suggests, in
writing about D. H. Lawrence, that "when the Other is obliterated, the
individual is also obliterated. . . . He . . . exhibits a deep unshakable faith in
the inexplicable processes of life—or fate, or time, or accident—against
which the individual must assert himself in a continued struggle." Emotion
battles reason, overwhelming the limited narrowness of rational thought
and design. As Waller suggests, "The paranoid search for material security
is the external sign of inner restlessness born of the dream of an America

permanent only in its changes and chances." Such conflict permeates the very being of man, that terrible opposition which Oates discusses in regard to Schopenhauer between "the will and the idea, the blind primitive force of will, or life, and the enlightened, would-be autonomous force of the intellect. The struggle is dramatic and endless. . . . man splits in two, drawn by the erotic in one direction and by the principles of the mind in another, unable to synthesize the two." Manichean dualism lacerates man's self-consciousness. The will seeks its own triumphant isolation and in so doing generates its own self-destruction. The Christian idea of losing the self, of propelling one's self beyond dualistic design in order to find it, becomes the apocalyptic equilibrium of annihilation, liberation, and surrender. As Walter Sullivan asserts, "The modern hero, placed irrevocably beyond good and evil, must create himself. The necessity for self-creation is at once his doom and his only avenue to freedom; he must transcend his own society and in the process he will destroy himself."

"I feel that my own place is to dramatize the nightmares of my time," Oates explains, "and (hopefully) to show how some individuals find a way out, awaken, come alive, move into the future." The nightmares of women as victims, urban slums, and isolated selves in most cases overwhelm the possibility of an individual's awakening. Passion almost precludes knowledge, nearly obscures self-recognition in its ferocity and tumble. If, as Oates suggests, "all literature deals with a contest of wills," what we have in her huge novels has a kinship with Poe, with his enclosed worlds and the rage within, the vampiric wills battling one another to the point of life and death. Imps of the perverse stalk her fictions, as they clutter Hugh Petrie's blurred consciousness in *The Assassins* (1975). Reality—whatever it is—emerges in gothic garb, lurid and passionate in its stare, as in *Mysteries of Winterthurn*. "Gothicism, whatever it is, is not a literary tradition so much as a fairly realistic assessment of modern life," Oates insists, and, in insisting, reveals the Manichean manic tone and style of her art. If the gothic can be defined as an awareness of another interior or spiritual realm, usually demonic and terrible in its essence and conscious of human decay and irrationality, then certainly Oates's fiction, however naturalistic in appearance, is essentially gothic. Add to this her eye for the grotesque, a form of modern gothic literature in which the "normal" is elusive and the misshapen and isolated are central to the character, plot, and setting, and you approach the fierce center of her haunted mind. Her comments on Dostoyevski reveal the added dimensions of power in her own work: "Dostoevski's imagination is such that he conceives the kernel of his drama as a conflict within the parts of one self. . . . his psychological insights deal mainly with the self-lacerating effects of egoism and its corollary, the wish for destruction and death." We are left admiring "the splendid unpredictability of the writer as writer, who can *leave nothing unsaid,* whose imagination is so nervously rich that characters and ideas multiply themselves as if by their own volition."

How can an artist with such a vision harness such a torrential flow? Oates's earlier novels, discussed in detail by other critics, rely essentially on third-person narrative. That particular form has led several critics to misinterpret her essential vision and to claim her as kin to Dreiser or, in some outrageous cases, William Dean Howells! Some more perceptive interpreters recognized the truth of the matter: "Oates' early fiction is clearly in the dominant American fictional tradition of romance, derived from Hawthorne and beyond. . . . It insists predominantly upon atmosphere and action, and upon a constant use of allegorical, mythical, and symbolic devices to point the reader beyond the surface action." As Oates acknowledges, "It *is* a good time to be an imaginative writer. Most writers today are free of the necessity of telling a story in a conventional manner; now we are able to use fantasy and surrealism and even mythic and fairy-tale elements in our art." One critic even goes so far to suggest that *them,* her award-winning novel, is in fact a parody of naturalism.

In any case, with the earlier exception of *Expensive People* (1968), by the time of *The Assassins* and *Childwold* (1976) Oates had begun to experiment with more open-ended fiction, fiction recounted from the point of view of the characters themselves. The first-person interior monologue replaces the third-person more objective narrative angle of vision. Mystery enters the more romantic mode of the confession; the self imposes its own order upon the world around it more readily or at least more visibly, trapped within certain egos, certain minds, and the naturalistic or more realistic perspectives surrender to the "up-front" obsessions of these characters. Reality—the character's angle of vision—constantly threatens to fragment and shatter, always outracing the mind's abilities to comprehend it: "Reality is constantly turning into something else; simplicity breaks up into fragments, baffling us; nothing stays, nothing is permanent; characters who are defined in one way break loose and assume deeper, vaster dimensions. . . . what is intended to be a parable or prophecy . . . becomes a great mystic work in which all man's acts, whether 'good' or 'evil,' are held finally to be of little account."

Such a vision consistently threatens the patterns Oates the artist intends to create, and in several cases shatters the work itself. When consciousness consumes itself and the palpable physical world is swallowed up within the bloated blur of that babbling consciousness, as in *The Assassins* and *Angel of Light* (1981), Oates's later novels become monotonous, tedious, and inert. They fail under their own convoluted weight. When she has a firmer grasp on some wider reality, some more palpable design, where her characters' self-consciousness is in league with some "other" world, some suggestion of an "other" realm—contemporary America, myth, religion, whatever—as in the novels *The Triumph of the Spider Monkey* (1976) and *Son of the Morning* (1978), her novels succeed. And when—at last!—the Manichean vision emerges solidly within the romantic form it seems destined to inhabit, as in the magnificent *Bellefleur* (1980), Oates not only achieves her masterpiece—so far—but masters in full force her authentic voice.

Bobbie Gotteson, the handsome maniac who plays guitar, wishes for a screen test, and desires only "to be a face on a billboard," inverts standard Christian and American values in his frenzied confession in *The Triumph of the Spider Monkey* with almost as much fervor and perverse pleasure as Richard Everett, who subverts the suburban values of *Expensive People*. He is the mad isolato, a grotesque creature whose name ironically mimics his isolation and whose very existence indicts and at the same time appears to be an extension of the values that come under attack. His "gnosis" emerges in his strong will, his apparent ability (so he thinks) to bend others to his psychic powers: "I felt my powers rise and flow over, like light if light could turn into water, fountains of water." It follows then that "God is a Maniac like me," even though finally "I was out-guessed by the God of Night." And all the time he explains that his insanity is merely a pose, a way of keeping his inviolate self intact: "And so I pretended madness, to save myself from disaster. Yet I was always sane. I am like you: a progression of states of mind, forms of sanity that keep moving and eluding definition. I was always sane and had practiced insanity." In this essential image of himself, the Manichean vision of the book takes root.

Gotteson makes quite clear, like Nathanael Vickery after him, that his true self exists in the realm of the spirit. The body disgusts him. When murder takes over, the hacking of nine women, "my body took over, and when bodies take over the spirit sails over the horizon." This irreconcilable split, fiercely schizophrenic and at the same time reflecting the American society of which he considers himself a part—heading west, longing for a career as a songwriter and singer in the style of "Sloe-Eyed Gypsy, American"—rages throughout the book. Hate and pity emerge from one another. His own rage fuels his music, as if the latter could in some way soothe the former. Thoughts come as convulsions; ideas appear to be spasms. His handsome body momentarily hides a mad spirit. His career in films becomes a pornographic circus, the height of his art being "Seventeen Mannequins

and a Guy," in which he sexually assaults and then dismembers with a
machete seven female dummies. Events slide into hallucinations and vice-
versa. Prison for him represents the inside of experience; everything else
exists outside, and, as in America in the seventies, "the Outside styles ap-
proximated the Inside spirit." All death for Bobbie is suicide, even if it be
murder. Even the assassination of President Kennedy enrages him: "*It made
me want to kill someone.*" Whether he is the norm or the subversion of the
norm, he can no longer tell, muddying the impenetrable Manichean waters
of his consciousness: "I couldn't come from anything normal or good. . . .
But since everything in the world comes from the world and is normal and
good, I must be somehow normal and good."

Oates structures the novel along traditional Christian lines. The first of
twenty chapters is entitled "Nativity," the final chapter, "Redemption."
Out of darkness into light he is born, although he is found in Locker 79-C
in the main waiting room of the Trailways Bus Terminal on Canal Street in
New York City. Each chapter, like an emblematic episode in a romance,
provides a glimpse of Gotteson's life. Each appears in a series of "jumpshots,
athletic tricks of the camera, montage-freezings," as "An Unfilmed Love
Scene," "Unrehearsed Interview," "How the Maniac Gotteson Travelled
West," "Why I Hacked," and "Gotteson's Pilot-Film": the detritus of modern media—news items, psychological explanations, scenes from a lost script.
Each functions as a kind of failed epiphany, a microcosm of Gotteson's
mind and the state of the materialistic world around him that values sex,
Hollywood careers, and the superficiality of all things.

Several people throughout his life call him a monkey because of his
dark hair, his inhuman exploits, his athletic and sexual abilities. The final
Manichean triumph: spider monkey overrides the human beings to the
point where Gotteson declares only half in jest, "I told them I was in essence
a Spider Monkey, in my soul, with a looping furry cunning tail scrunched up
inside my trousers." Oates's vision is complete. The Manichean trap clamps
shut.

The novel as confession approximates the realm of the romance. An
individual self wrestling with particular problems projects himself upon the
world around him. The reader views an almost allegorical realm surrounding that central self. Gotteson appears doomed from the start: the world on
the "outside" and the "inside" allows no escape, no place for any possibility
of self-transcendence or recognition. Rather, a Manichean realm presses
relentlessly against him, driving him inward, outward, beyond the pale. As
a boy he is buggered by blacks in New Jersey; his therapist calls him an ugly
monkey and declares he'll kill someone someday; his own rage is driven

inward with no place to go. Interior violence broods and festers. A prison dentist gives him no Novocain while lambasting his appearance and his status as a prisoner; Melva, the aged mistress who picks him up, promises him screen tests and recording sessions but only delivers more sex, while he chauffeurs her around Hollywood. Prison warps him. His "old man" there, Danny Minxs, buggers him in front of the other inmates as punishment and power play to subdue him, rails against women, infects Bobbie with his own "psychic powers," and deserts him on their way west. The world of El Portal, a Hollywood estate overlooking the sea, promises only more parties and sex, and Melva and her crew egg him on to climb up on the house like a trained monkey. He falls; they laugh; Melva offers him a stooge role in a television comedy. There is nowhere to turn in a progressively sadistic world.

Gotteson's quest goes nowhere except into the darker realm of murder, and even then it seems to him the machete is acting by itself. "It sliced up more people. . . . this frightened me because my soul blacked out at such times and abandoned me to whatever was going on." Time "collapsed into itself." A sense of doom and dark shadows hovers everywhere.

Gothic romance lies at the heart of Gotteson's compulsive, obsessive behavior, as if the confessional novel, mirroring more the internal world of emotions than the external world of social conventions, had entered the realm of the romance in the dark terms of some of Hawthorne's self-obsessed characters. One critic suggested that Hawthorne's characters resembled Poe's, except that Hawthorne's appeared in his own third-person narration, while many of Poe's demonic creatures relied upon the first-person confession to reveal their lurid tales. Oates demonstrates her ability to conjure up Poe's world in word and deed here.

All the elements of romance are here, submerged in Gotteson's first-person confession: the withdrawn settings, the episodic, dreamlike nature of the plot, the mix of light and dark, the self at the center of the narrative, the visible author at work—and the ongoing unravelling of various compulsions, obsessions, guilts. And if ever a vision was founded on Manichean polarities, this certainly has its palpable designs on us.

If pity had not claimed him, Gotteson explains, "my life would not be this disjointed confession, but a series of haunting melodies joined to lyric language." The language of the book, while not exactly lyric, certainly embodies the hypnotic spell of most romances. Here it begins:

Noise, vibrations, murmuring nosey crowd of bastards with nothing else to do but gawk—grunting sweating bastard in a

uniform reaching in and grabbing me out of the darkness and
delivering me to light—
    —to lights, that is—
Holding me up to those lights. *A baby! A baby still alive!*
Time: 6:05 PM. Date: February 14, 1944.

Sensations precede thought. The style lurches forward, filled with repetitions, as if consciousness were trying to grasp what was going on—"light—
lights—lights—." Ellipses break the flow, increase that sense of grappling
with circumstance and event. Italics preach astonishment at what is happening. Long hypnotic paragraphs shatter, stumble onto sudden short sentences. The jerkiness of the rhetoric again reveals the teetering consciousness
trying to maintain control and pursue understanding. Facts seem cursory,
beside the point, almost ironically tossed in. The date of Gotteson's birth is
the least important item here, other than the fact that it connects him and
his future life with specific, however shadowy, American reality and historical moment.

Oates shares Faulkner's power, but her style only superficially resembles his. Faulkner never abandons his sense of place, the habits and notions
of a peculiarly southern mind: a Balzacian reality lurks within the circuitous
rush of rhetoric. In Oates regions blur. Mind and matter tremble, fuse,
separate. Language attaches itself to the direct emotions and states of mind
of a particular character. The outside world, however recreated with a
Dreiserian thirst for details, remains vague, curiously distant, remote. In her
less successful novels, as we shall see, it entirely evaporates, leaving the
reader within a convoluted rhetoric that swallows itself and dissolves everything within and beyond it. Dream precedes history in Oates's vision:
"We seek the absolute dream. We are forced back continually to an acquiescence in all that is hallucinatory and wasteful." Finally Oates shatters the
hypnotic circuitousness of a Faulkner by breaking the line, injecting gasps,
italics, curiously random facts and figures. This exaggerates the character's
isolation, his distance from any known world, his Manichean entrapment
within himself.

Melville, Oates has written, sought not the equilibrium of opposites,
the balanced art of alternative positions—his famous "contraries"—but a
nihilistic destruction of tension. Of *The Confidence-Man* she writes, "The
underlying motif of the novel is not just the tension of antipodal forces but
rather the fact of no tension—of a final nihilism." Evil does not triumph
over good; the struggle between good and evil is eradicated. "For a writer
whose aim is to penetrate into a 'basic truth,' the sustainment of any two

points of view will suggest, in the end, the mockery of assigning to one of two antithetical views a positiveness worthy of one's faith—worthy of one's life. The quest ends, ideally, in the negation and not in the compromise or resolution of tension in Melville's irreconcilable world of opposites; it is at once a transcendence and an annihilation."

At the conclusion of *The Triumph of the Spider Monkey,* Gotteson remains by the side of his final dying victim. He has already foreshadowed his murder of Doreen B., his last murder, by referring to it as "that revelation." As his anger slowly leaves him, reflecting the blood leaving her body, he thinks, "I began to panic that she would die before she could explain." Death mirrors a purity, a place of not-female and not-male, of the not-human (in contrast to the all-too-grisly humanity of his own experience), an almost religious place which Gotteson has sought but never found. His murders he describes as his victims' suicides: he releases them from the horror he has lived. As Doreen dies, she utters, "I can see into it. . . ." Gotteson's violent act becomes for him a final act of self-definition and self-destruction. He realizes suddenly that he is one whole person, a horror in his own right: "He is Gotteson the Spider Monkey and nobody else is Gotteson and Gotteson cannot get born into being anyone else, Gotteson is Gotteson is Gotteson forever." The splintered fragments of his confession coalesce in this chilling shock of recognition. Manichean dualisms shatter and leave behind "Gotteson Inside, Gotteson Outside . . . all's one Gotteson Gotteson Gotteson unrepeatable. There you are." He screams for an ambulance: "It isn't too late, help me!"

Transcendence and annihilation erupt simultaneously. It is at once "a penitential act. A Negative Act. An undoing-of-Magic Act." In a sense he has earned his final humanity, however terrible it is. He is capable of anything. The self becomes an act of horror. He is us. It is not here a nihilistic act. Gotteson seems to recognize what has happened, what a creature he is: he calls for help. We can see the final cry as an act of both despair and liberation. But he at once recognizes both, as no one else in the book has or can. Manicheism may not have been so much transcended as ineradicably fused, the same kind of horrifying interpenetration of opposites that frightened Hawthorne. In any case it seems to be the point that Oates longs for in her fictions, the pinnacle of her vision, freighted at once with deliverance and disintegration. In such a violent landscape, however, both inside and outside, it is indeed the spider monkey's triumph.

Selfhood and the physical world are always threatened by submergence in the manic sensationalism of Oates's style. When this happens, voices wail in a void and turn tedious and unrelated to anything but their own garrulous chatter. The physical world evaporates, blurs; everything dissolves;

emotions turn vaporous; vertigo takes over. In such instances Oates sounds as though she were hyperventilating, awash in a babble of ellipses and dashes, a Jamesian "talking head" gone mad. Frenzied fragments don't so much dance as congeal, echoes reverberate off other echoes, and a rhetorical stupor prevails. Such is the case in *Angel of Light* and *The Assassins*.

As a point of contrast, here is the opening of Updike's *Rabbit, Run:* "Boys are playing basketball around a telephone pole with a blackboard bolted to it. Legs, shouts. The scrape and snap of Keds on loose alley pebbles seems to catapult their voices high into the moist March air blue above the wires." Images prevail, hard and pure, so much so that the observing self is practically submerged in the physical reality of the world.

In *The Assassins* in a similar scene the opposite is true: "Basketball court, midwinter. Boys running loose. Like dogs, like colts, like deer. Black boys—of high school age mainly—a single white boy, no more than thirteen—shouting and darting from side to side—the basketball bouncing at odd unpredictable angles from the uneven surface of cracked asphalt—yells, screams, shouts of joy—disappointment—sudden rage—and then joy again, and again the pounding of feet." Here the sensations of the event take over. The concrete images, many of them tumbled upon one another, are submerged in the sheer rush of the event. So much is piled on that the event itself is heavily submerged in the experienced sensations of it.

This paragraph suggests the general nature of the style in *The Assassins*. Manicheism reigns: dreaming and waking, light and dark, God and the Devil, truth and lies. "The Petries have chosen improbable mates, they've been guided more by romance than by reason [revealing] *a bizarre inclination toward the precarious, the forbidden, the wobbling, the dizzy.*" But as Friedman suggests, the novel registers only "the complete isolation of the individual in his personality."

Hugh, the grotesque cartoonist, babbles relentlessly about art, death, jokes. His own impotence shatters his fragile ego, although the reader is aware of such impotence by the sheer repetitious breathlessness of his ponderous probing. Yvonne Radek, poor orphan, widow of the dead Andrew, falls numb, exudes a glacial calm, imagines her own murder at the hands of a crazed ax-man. Stephen pursues religious mysticism, a bodiless, timeless trance that reduces the world and everyone in it to unimportant ciphers, distant presences. All in their own way remain detached, self-conscious, paranoid, obsessed, and each detests the body. They are all Manicheans, prisoners of an ineradicable, feverish self-consciousness that worships a tenuous self-control, a querulous celebration of "the intellect and the precise measurements, its setting-up of empires, word by word by word, which nothing could demolish." All this babble turns in upon itself, making the novel almost unreadable, a sterile vacuum of stupefied stuttering.

We can see what Oates is up to, a theme that will emerge triumphant in *Bellefleur*. The original Petrie—"petrified," Hugh calls his older brother Andrew—fled England in the 1600s and became "a deranged Puritan minister—famous for the transactions viciousness can make with civilization." He was "a zealous preacher of the Word, a nonconforming, stubborn, querulous hero who braved the Atlantic Ocean with other maniacs." Andrew is the modern-day Petrie, a right-wing political theorist who quits politics to write his supreme opus, praising legalism over anarchy, a masterful public speaker and public presence who casts his giant shadow across the lives of Hugh, Yvonne, and Stephen, the remaining triptych of the novel, maimed by the Petrie "curse." Andrew is aware of the problem: "The Puritans were capable of extraordinary acts of courage . . . because they were so certain of themselves, their own conscience. They were fanatics. . . . Their only problem was that they were deluded, as we know: they thought it was God directing them, but in fact it was history." This is Hawthorne's territory, the god of romance battling with the history of the novel.

In Andrew's time the Word has degenerated into words. Puritan self-control and God-obsessive people have "petrified." "An abstract tower of words" casts its distorted shadow over the entire book. Creation becomes concept; image becomes idea: "The words are always the same words but changed, turned upside down, reversed, they are mirror images of one another and we are mirror images of one another." Oates has fallen into the very abyss she warns us of: her "attack" on consciousness, on words, on intellect sinks under the weight of these characters' consciousness, their omnivorous, emasculating words. The image of the Petrie family is there—America in microcosm, Puritan certainty shattered and dispersed—but it gets lost in the monotonous monologues of the Petrie survivors. It is not that the characters scrutinized are too abnormal to identify with (as one critic suggests, a "ranting psychotic, a suicidal public figure, a frigid schizoid, a drifting mystic"); it is their unrelieved talk that does them in.

Oates has a significant point. Consciousness itself is the ultimate assassin. Ego kills. Even Andrew, in love with motion and power, sinks into depressive stasis and in doing so at last contrives his own suicide to look like an assassination. Consciousness prides itself on conjuring up its own apocalyptic demise, caught up in "the romance of disaster, sheer catastrophe . . . to want to believe suddenly and irrevocably that all was lost." Hugh attempts suicide; Yvonne hallucinates about her own dismemberment; Stephen, like Alice through the looking glass, drifts away from language into abject silence. The end of the novel reveals "the Devil whom you cast down a thousand years into that bottomless hole." The beast arises; apocalypse now: "I am the way, the tooth the might." But Stephen is correct to repudiate such babble; he remains willing to accommodate himself to anything, a glimpse of resurrection and perseverance.

"One must be connected to the world," Andrew Petrie tells Stephen, "but how?—how? They don't tell us." When Oates is disconnected from the world, her vision blurs. Rhetoric clamors but rings hollow. No amount of screaming will help. All rings false.

In *Son of the Morning* (the title is taken from the *Book of the Prophet Isaiah*, 14:12–15, and refers to the devil), Oates succeeds once again with the form of the confessional novel, sustained and enlarged by the distinctive elements of romance. The book's three chapters and epilogue parallel the Christian pattern once again: "The Incarnation," "The Witness," "Last Things," and "The Sepulcher." The text itself represents Nathanael Vickery's testament, his "desperate prayer" to God, "an utterance of faith, of infinite faith," looking back on his failed career as a charismatic preacher, presently waiting for God's presence to show itself anew, left waiting forever in his own private sepulcher: "Yet there was, there is, no *we:* there is only an *I.*" Recounting his life he recounts his vision and like the romancer envisions a world as a self-projection of that vision.

Vickery's quest reflects Wesley Kort's analysis of religiously pluralistic American society. Kort suggests that for religious pluralism to exist, people must agree to a common nonreligious life, a public domain where no one religion may dominate. Consequently, society constructs this nonreligious domain; it becomes the unifying influence upon, the identifying mark of that society; and it relies upon the language of logic, of rational, empirical verification, to uphold it. As a result the depersonalization of society's members must triumph, leaving no place for the personal or the religious. Therefore a split results in American society between the private and the public, between immanent mystery and solvable problem, retreat and work, the "religious-withdrawn" and the "nonreligious engaged." Kort sees many confessional novels (he cites several of Updike's) as opportunities to attempt to heal this basic American division, "a torn world in which two goods are separated from one another, in which two self-enclosed worlds are unrelated." The problem itself is Manichean. So too is Oates's "solution."

One other important organizational and structural device holds *Son of the Morning* together. In his lifetime Vickery experiences seven visions, "seven revelations of extraordinary magnitude . . . seven small crucifixions." These visions not only reveal Nathan's character development and the mad escalation of his faith; they also establish a decisive pattern throughout the novel and give it the kind of organic shape that *The Assassins* lacks. And they suggest the scaffold epiphanies that organize Hawthorne's romances.

Nathan progresses—or regresses, as the case may be—from a vision of radiance and light at the age of five, fondling snakes in a fundamentalist church service, to a sixth vision in which he envisions himself as God, the two of them inseparable, to the seventh and final vision of utter collapse and withdrawal at the age of thirty-four (a year older than Christ at his death) on—Oates's marvelous touch—August 8, 1974, the day Richard Nixon resigned from the presidency. At eight he enters a trance when his father rejects his "Christ-madness"; at twelve he bites off a chicken's head to humble his aspiring pride; at nineteen he knifes out an eye during a sermon as penance for the reassertion of pride and lust. At twenty-six he perceives an overwhelming oneness wherein he himself is above sin and Christ is eclipsed. These epiphanies focus the self-escalation of the book, both structurally and thematically.

And what is Nathan's vision? Pure Manicheism reigns supreme again. Christ had no body; he was just a spirit. The spirit of the Lord is not bound up in the flesh in any manner or form; the Devil rules flesh, distorting our vision to accommodate it: "The Devil wants us to think that Jesus Christ was really a man and that he really died. . . . Before my fleshly being came into the world, *I* was." The senses, the will: these incorporate sin. "The only reality is the interior and invisible." Grace becomes the "cessation of all duality," for there can be none when only spirit is genuine. Vickery's vision eradicates Christ, "a mere image of God," and hurries toward destruction of that thin membrane between the fullness of an invisible spirit and the consequent emptiness if that spirit should withdraw. His horror during that final vision is to recognize "the odd ineffable *reality* of what was outside him." God shatters, "broken and separated into parts, into individuals, into people, 'men' and 'women' and 'children.' " It is a vision he cannot bear.

Of course Nathan's vision reflects the outer world of his narrative, or more particularly that outer world reflects his vision of it. His grandparents, by whom he was raised, reflect the Manichean design: Opal hungers for the spirit of the fundamentalist Christian; Dr. Thaddeus, a man of science, views the universe in strictly materialistic terms: "There is no spiritual world, only a materialistic world in which soul and mind are evolved with the body, grow old with the body, ail with the body, and finally die with the body's death. There is nothing permanent." His refuge resides in stoicism: "Better the vanquishment of all desire and all strife. The cessation of instinct itself." We inhabit only "a universe of change, flowing about us, flooding against us, bearing us away. Only the present moment is real."

The plot of the novel erupts along Manichean lines. The Vickerys' daughter is raped while returning from a church service; she becomes Nathan's mother. William Japheth Sproul III, Princeton graduate in a family of divines, becomes Nathan's disciple, but his eagerness and devotion suggest homosexual compulsion. He tries to murder Vickery, then commits suicide. Nathan's own lusts for the daughter of his eventual boss, the Reverend Marian Miles Boloff, drive him toward his outrageous faith in the spirit. And of course his spiritual faith appears to unbelievers as a "gospel of hate! Of regressive disdain for human relationships!"

Oates's America bristles with Manichean urges. Americans "are hungry for a true prophet, for a *true* evangelistic voice." Imagine Pentecostals thriving in Boston in 1965! And "in the early seventies it seemed as if everyone was hungry for this teaching. Salvation had nothing to do with social responsibility or action of any kind; it had nothing to do with human relationships." Middle-class youth turn from drugs to their own self-absorbed Christ. The landscape is ready in this "Age of Non-belief . . . materialistic, skeptical, blinded, atheistic. . . . Satan was the secret god of America." Which came first, Nathan's vision or the America he inhabits? And does his destruction suggest some wider apocalypse?

The elements of romance clearly haunt Nathan Vickery's confession: the allegorical characters inhabiting the design of flesh and spirit; the hypnotic style of the seven revelations, beautifully rendered by Oates at her rhetorical best; the episodic, dreamlike visitations and emblematic scenes; the emotional tenor and power of certain compulsions, obsessions, and guilts that seem to dictate the characters' every move. And in that strange opening scene in which Ashton Vickery contemplates shooting a pack of wild dogs ravaging the countryside (Manicheism at full cry) we get the strange, eerie setting of romance: "Only a peculiar glowering light that was like moonlight, like mist. . . . Like sleep, it was; like the dreamless sleep of the depths of the night. Perhaps he was sleeping?—dreaming? . . . and the pallid, dissolving Chautauqua Mountains and the oppressive sky itself . . . mesmerizing . . . drawn . . . into the vast silence, thinking that this had happened before: many times: and would happen many times again . . . everything he touched was an extension of himself." Nathan, now William, is left in his private sepulcher, waiting for a God who will not return, almost as if Oates were waiting for that full-blown romantic vision and form to come forth once and for all, out into the open, complete. In *Bellefleur* it finally does.

In *The Assassins* one of the characters comments, "Fairy tales are exactly analogous to life as it is lived in the family." In *Bellefleur* that astute observation becomes structure. Romance embodies Oates's Manichean vision in that splendid opening paragraph: "It was many years ago in that dark, chaotic, unfathomable pool of time before Germaine's birth . . . on a night in late September stirred by innumerable frenzied winds, like spirits contending with one another . . . that Mahalaleel came to Bellefleur Manor on the western shore of the great Lake Noir. . . ." The opening suggests *Absalom, Absalom!* in its pacing and poetic accretions. Time is distant; space is distant; the "neutral territory" all but announces its dominance. And spirits are already contending with one another, intimations of Leah and Gideon's marriage—"their love was too ravenous to be contained by their mortal bodies." Lake Noir suggests Poe; the name Mahalaleel suggests strange spirits, magic omens, haunted demons.

Bellefleur spawns "disturbing labyrinthian tales. . . . The living and the dead. Braided together. Woven together. An immense tapestry taking in centuries . . . a dizzying profusion of plots . . . calculations, aspirations, dreams—some of them . . . quite mad . . . stories, tales, anecdotes set in the mountains, which no one quite believed and could not quite disregard." Oates shares the "simple frank astonishment at the pathways others' lives took" with her huge canvas of characters, the sheer torrent of tales and tellers: dwarfs, beasts, feuds, mass murders, mystics, doomed romances, transformations, disappearances, ghosts, prophecies, rapes, celebrations: the Bellefleur clan as all of American history, of the American psyche. Many brood on strange obsessions, linked to objects of their rapt devotions: Leah and her huge spider Love, Noel's vial of poison, Jedediah's submission to Mt. Blanc, Raphael's mystic awe for Mink Pond, Samuel's disappearance into the Turquoise Room, "the room of contamination." Strange attachments, mystical unions, obsessed alliances create a fairy-tale world, a nightmare realm, in which objects assume emblematic powers. The world speaks in omens; events double, spawn unforeseen consequences, spill over into inner tormented souls. Here is the American-Manichean "ethos" raised to its romantic heights, its metamorphic triumph.

Worlds split, mirror one another. The palpable physical world of Oates's Adirondack region prompts astonishment: "What maddened mind, deranged by an unspeakable lust, had imagined all this into being?" In such a world chronological order collapses; Bellefleurs show only contempt at such linear notions of time and consequence: "Everything shifts, changes, grows fluid, transparent." And at the same time the turmoil of the mysterious interior world—the true world of Hawthorne's romance—continues and thrives unabated, "a universe simultaneous with this universe . . . a shadow-world, a mirror-world." Both are beautifully balanced; neither eradicates the other, though the demonic inner world colors the exterior landscape around Lake Noir. Of *The Brothers Karamazov* Oates speaks of "a double of itself contained in its most brilliant of pages, a kind of shadow or antinovel whose tragedy mocks the positive accomplishments of the larger, Christian work." She could as well be describing *Bellefleur,* though here the world of gothic romance overshadows the Christian parallels and dimensions. Her characters pass in and out through "slits in the fabric of time," inhabiting that "dark, chaotic, unfathomable pool" of romance, spaces between exterior and interior worlds, one reflecting the other, a territory not so much neutral as nightmarishly realized.

Parallels abound to parallel these worlds. In the first eight chapters Oates shifts between present and past times, between the birth of Germaine in the present and Jedediah's retreat to the mountains in 1806 and 1809. Jedediah withdraws because he is drawn to the young wife, Germaine, of his younger brother Louis. In the present, Leah awaits the birth of her daughter Germaine. In 1825 Germaine alone survives the mass murder of the original Bellefleur, Jean-Pierre, her husband Louis, and their three children, and eventually marries the "reformed" mystic Jedediah: they generate the Bellefleur family tree, the somber, sexless survivor and the religious fanatic. And of the three surviving Bellefleurs after the destruction of the Manor and everyone within it, two are ancient women; the other is Germaine, age four.

Bellefleur represents both a historical family, interwoven with American history, a state of soul, the exterior world of ambition, action, the "lust of acquisition," the pursuit of money and power, and the interior world of consciousness, reflection, the lust for solitude and retreat, the pursuit of some uncontaminated place or the sweetness of pure revenge. It suggests Emerson's mystic materialism or materialistic mysticism, that curious American amalgam.

History reveals the abuse of Indians, tenant farmers, blacks, and fruitpickers, the acquisition of land, empire-building, frontier violence, family feuds, regional fracases. The official attitude of the Bellefleur clan in this regard "was one of robust jocularity. . . . Nothing so important it can't be laughed away. Shouted away." These early men suggest Faulkner's southerners in their "passion for gambling . . . their reckless, inventive challenges, and for their courtesy and grace in defeat." "Only in motion is there life," Gideon declares in his pursuit of cars, horses, women, planes. "The notion of *thinking,* of withdrawing oneself from action in order to systematically *think,* struck him as not only unmanly but implausible: for how could one force oneself to think, merely *think,* when the world awaited!"

Jean-Pierre's arrival in America parallels American legends and myths. He envisions "forests of prodigious beauty . . . streams visibly crowded with salmon and trout, a virgin wilderness ripe for exploitation," diamonds and rubies and sapphires and great blocks of jade in the soil, and silver and gold deposits of a lushness never seen before on earth. "We are all Americans now," declares Raphael, Jedediah's son, a millionaire ten times over—who will have his skin stripped and made into the covering of a drum after his death, whose vast lands Leah plots to regain in present time, a prophecy she feels resides within daughter Germaine's strange psychic powers. And for these Americans, the first Jean-Pierre, banished from France, "repudiated by his own father . . . the past simply ceased to exist." American myth is symbolized by the Bellefleur coat of arms, "a falcon volant, a snake draped about its neck": power, exploitation, isolation, the triumph of the self in pastless natural paradise, acquiring "in the 1770's, some 2,889,500 acres of wilderness land for seven and a half pence an acre." Hawthorne's Pyncheons. Faulkner's Sutpen.

But there is the shadow-world, the state of soul, the Manichean Bellefleur curse, "an unfortunate combination of passion and melancholy . . . a propensity for energy and passion that might be countered at any time by a terrifying bleakness, a queer emptiness of vision": man deprived of history in a dark uncertain wilderness of his own making, the demonic side of the American Adam, the gothic loneliness. "Indeed, the spirit of contention was sometimes thought to be the essential curse of the Bellefleurs—for isn't it out of contention that all evils spring?" "Spirits contending with one another": the solitude of Jedediah's withdrawal to the mountains, Vernon's metaphysical poetry, Raphael's pond, the passionate brutality of Leah and Gideon's marriage. This is a world where death constantly threatens, where a God of Destruction broods and watches, a world of grudges and revenge. "For revenge . . . makes war against what is fixed. It is always revolutionary. It cannot exert itself but must *be* exerted; and exerted only through violence, by a selfless individual who is willing to die in the service of his mission." Gideon crashes his plane into Bellefleur Manor, killing them all on Germaine's fourth birthday, at once a supreme Bellefleurian act of pride, tragedy, revenge, suicide, and self-righteous self-destruction.

Oates's haunted mind has at last produced the romance she has seemed on the verge of producing from the beginning. Bellefleur Manor, like the Pyncheon House or Sutpen's Hundred, symbolizes the entire Bellefleur saga, "with its innumerable walls and towers and turrets and minarets, like a castle composed in a feverish sleep, when the imagination leapt over itself, mad to outdo itself, growing more frantic and greedy." Time twists and coils in that psychic inner realm of the romance, as Oates assures us in her author's note: "*Bellefleur* is a region, a state of the soul, and it does exist; and there, sacrosanct, its laws are utterly logical." Shades of Hawthorne's prefaces, apologizing, defending his fictional creation. Some tales soar; others dissipate. Style can turn both monotonous and riveting, can be "overwrought and exaggerated and unhealthy." But it is the sheer scope and power of Oates's *Bellefleur* that triumphs. At this point in her prodigious career it is her masterpiece. And as such it reflects, comments upon, extends, and achieves the kind of romance Hawthorne would have celebrated. Form and content, vision and voice match as splendidly as in Faulkner's *Absalom, Absalom!* Exorcism assumes romantic embodiment. At one point in the book, Oates quotes at length from Wordsworth's *The Prelude,* entranced herself, one would guess, by "something far more deeply interfused. . . . A motion and a spirit, that impels / All thinking things, all objects of all thought, / And rolls through all things." Her spirit shares Hawthorne's darker compulsions and angle of vision. And in *Bellefleur* it "impels" her darker vision of the soul with an artistic integrity and authority that astounds.

ELAINE SHOWALTER

Joyce Carol Oates: A Portrait

"For a serious American writer—especially for a woman writer," Joyce Carol Oates told an interviewer in 1980, "this is by far the best era in which to live." Certainly the eighties have seen the extraordinary flowering of Oates's protean talent. This year has already seen the publication of a new novel, and her classic short story about female adolescence, "Where Are You Going, Where Have You Been?" has been made into a sensitive film, "Smooth Talk," by the feminist director Joyce Chopra. Yet despite her position as one of the most versatile and intellectually powerful of contemporary American writers, and despite the series of important books on female experience she has written especially during this decade, Oates has never had the acknowledgment from feminist readers and critics that she deserves.

Her newest and most intensely moving novel, *Marya: A Life,* published last month by Dutton, may change this pattern. It is a wrenching account of the development of a woman writer who reaches back to the wasteland of her brutal childhood to find the mother who has abandoned her, and to reclaim a matrilineage that is both painful and empowering. *Marya,* which insists on the woman writer's need to confront her female inheritance and to seek the lost mother although she may be as disturbing as she is comforting, is Oates's most personal statement about a female literary tradition, as well as the novel which presents her most compelling heroine.

In writing about Joyce Carol Oates, one must inevitably deal with the two issues that every critical discussion of her work has mentioned for

From *Ms.* 14, no. 9 (March 1986). © 1986 by Elaine Showalter.

twenty years: its "quantity" and its "violence." She is indeed extraordinar-
ily productive. Since 1964, when her first book appeared, Oates has published seventeen novels, thirteen volumes of short stories, eight collections
of poetry, five books of literary criticism, and two books of plays. Hundreds
of her short stories are still uncollected, and there are enough unpublished
novels waiting in her desk drawer to take her through the 1990s. This is an
impressive record, although many Victorian novelists, for example, equaled
or surpassed it (Anthony Trollope wrote forty-six novels, even George
Gissing, that hard-luck case, twenty-seven; but for a woman writer, critics
have hinted, such fecundity is positively indecent. One fierce novel and
consumption, or obscurity and a posthumous trunkful of poems in the attic,
seem more decorous for someone who is, after all, a *serious* writer. Some
criticism is plainly envious; Oates herself has noted that "perhaps critics
(mainly male) who charged me with writing too much are secretly afraid
that someone will accuse them of having done too little with their lives."

How does she do it? Oates leads a balanced but intensely disciplined
life, in which writing comes first. She lives with her husband of twenty-five
years, the editor and critic Raymond Smith, in a bright country house near
Princeton University, where she has been a Lecturer in Creative Writing
since 1978. She gets up very early, and stays up rather late, and writes for
several hours every day, most recently on a new IBM computer, which, she
says, feels like an extension of her brain waves.

Yet there is room in her life for other pleasures. She is sociable and
athletic, finding time in addition to her teaching and writing for a daily run
in the woods, and for gossipy lunches and long phone conversations with a
wide circle of women friends around Princeton and New York (including
novelist and film writer Eleanor Bergstein, the poet Alicia Ostriker, lawyer
Leigh Bienen, to whom *Marya* is dedicated, journalist Lucinda Franks, and
Princeton colleagues Sandra Gilbert and myself).

She keeps up a huge correspondence with fellow writers, both men and
women; serves on numerous committees for literature and the arts; and is a
frequent traveler and speaker on college campuses. She also does her own
housework and occasionally jokes that she will volunteer to wash windows
for less organized friends.

She does not, however, suffer fools or bores gladly, send Christmas
cards, bake or indeed eat cookies, or go shopping for clothes (I once persuaded her to come with me to a discount fashion store, a successful but
perhaps unique expedition during which she added a red mohair coat to a
wardrobe of clothes made and regularly mailed from Millerport, New
York, by her mother). Yet to say these things makes her sound like any

successful woman executive of the eighties, and she is most decidedly not like other people. In the midst of a quite ordinary conversation about the news or television or the family, Oates often inserts remarks whose philosophical penetration makes the rest of us feel like amoebas in the company of a more highly evolved life form. She seems to be someone who is never blocked, whose unconscious is always available, who is most alive when she is writing and working. She has the uncanny personal power of genius.

In the seventies, Oates's work was often criticized for its violent themes and images, for scenes of riots, beatings, and murders; and reviewers wondered whether some trauma of her own was responsible for her dark vision. Oates responded in a 1981 essay for the *New York Times Book Review*, called "Why Is Your Writing So Violent?" The question, she wrote, was "always insulting . . . always ignorant . . . always sexist," a question that would never be asked of a serious male artist. It came from the belief that women should limit their writing to the domestic and the subjective; that in a violent society and century, "war, rape, murder, and the more colorful minor crimes evidently fall within the exclusive province of the male writer, just as, generally, they fall within the exclusive province of male action."

In the early years of Oates's career (and recently in the aftermath of her much-publicized essay on boxing for the *New York Times Magazine*), critical shock at her violent imagination was often accompanied by surprise at her feminine appearance: could this delicate creature be the author of these powerful stories? Walter Clemons's comments in *Newsweek* are typical of the genre: "If you met her at a literary party and failed to catch her name, it might be hard to imagine her reading, much less writing, the unflinching fiction [of Joyce Carol Oates]." In the nineteenth century, women who wrote sensational fiction under pseudonyms, such as Rhoda Broughton, were sometimes forbidden by their fathers to read their own books.

Oates is not particularly gentle, as it happens; she is fast and tough, funny and outspoken, impatient with pomposity and cant. But it's not simply a question of getting her right, or of asking the *real* "Joyce Carol Oates" to stand up. Just as her name exists only for the title page of books (nobody calls her "Joyce Carol"), she has always insisted that the writer exists only in words, and that the contrast between the printed self—"revised tirelessly, monomaniacally . . . so that it is as close to perfection as possible"—and the private self—"mere flesh"—must always be disappointing. Oates has maintained that, for the woman writer, this split between the private and public identities must be even greater, since "when the writer is alone . . . with language," she experiences herself as genderless. Yet she has also acknowledged that the woman who writes "is a woman writer by others' definitions." Her appearance, her femininity, her conformity to a sexual identity that is socially defined, must be part of the world in which her work is judged.

Feminist critics have sometimes taken Oates's insistence that the imagination has no gender as a denial of her social identity as a woman writer, yet Oates's sense of herself as what she calls a "(woman) writer" has intensified during the eighties. It is not that she has abandoned or in any way simplified the complex intellectual allegiances to philosophy or classic literature that mark her writing, but that she has added to it an exchange with an equally complex female heritage. Oates's early relationship to the male literary tradition is most clearly presented in her book of short stories, *Marriages and Infidelities* (1972), in which she brilliantly reimagines and rewrites famous stories by Chekhov, Kafka, James, Joyce, and others. In an interview with Joe David Bellamy, Oates has explained that "these stories are meant to be autonomous stories, yet they are also testaments of my love and extreme devotion to these other writers; I imagine a kind of spiritual 'marriage' between myself and them."

Yet even within these literary "marriages" were the signs of infidelities: betrayals of theme, transgressions of form, transforming revisions of perspective that came from female experience. One story, "The Dead," is about the breakdown of Ilena Williams, a successful young novelist and teacher, whose anxiety, insomnia, and anorexia seem to signal her dis-ease with the male institutions of the univeristy, marriage, and literature.

These signs of rebellion and subversion within a framework of wifely devotion and service to a partriarchal tradition take on added meaning in the light of Oates's work since 1980, much of which has been a meditation from a dazzling variety of perspectives, on female creativity and female community. Her virtuoso fictional trilogy, *Bellefleur* (1980), *A Bloodsmoor Romance* (1982), and *Mysteries of Winterthurn* (1984), experiments with the female genres of the family chronicle, the romance, and the gothic. All explore what Oates has called the "on-going wrongs of women," from arranged marriages and domestic confinement to rape, sexual abuse, and incest. These novels also forge a bold alliance of male and female literary traditions, juxtaposing epigraphs and conventions from Louisa May Alcott, Emily Brontë, and Emily Dickinson, with those from Thoreau and Hawthorne.

In *Bloodsmoor*, a woman medium, "Deirdre of the Shadows," possessed by voices from the spirit world which she must translate, is Oates's representation of her own creative process. In *Mysteries of Winterthurn*, Oates invents both the character and the poems of a nineteenth-century woman writer much like Emily Dickinson, called "Iphigenia," and suggests through her narrative how much this woman, like her contemporaries, was sacrificed to patriarchal tyranny. While the novels satirically explore the more grandiose and blood-thirsty manifestations of patriarchal power, such as lynching, assassination, and nuclear weapons, they also suggest, through their interplay of "masculine" and "feminine" narrative conventions, how the plots and fantasies of the novel genre itself have invidiously wronged women.

In *Solstice* (1985), Oates turned away from these long historical novels to a brief chilling study of the relationship between two women. Utterly without sentimentality about female friendships, *Solstice* shows how the balance of power between the two women—one a famous painter, the other a teacher—is never resolved. Oates tells the story through the teacher, the weaker of the two, so that the artist remains always remote, inexplicable, frighteningly seductive, and dangerous. Without avoiding the erotic tension that bonds the women in sexual games and that drives each close to sickness and breakdown, Oates concentrates more on the drive for possession and dominance, the illusion of equality, in any love relationship.

Marya: A Life seems to bring these two strands of Oates's thought on the female tradition together. The heroine, Marya Knauer, is a brilliant writer who has been hurt and betrayed by both women and men. She is abandoned by her sluttish mother after her miner father's death when she is eight years old, an experience she will try to forget yet endlessly relive in dreams and in adult configurations of love and loss. She grows up with working-class relatives in the country along the Canal Road, where there are strange wild landscapes: the mother's wilderness, "nine miles of unpaved dirt and gravel . . . lush-growing scrub willow and oak and beech; the roadside wildflowers, chicory and Queen Anne's lace; patches of milkweed; poison ivy; pink sweetpeas"; and the father's wonderland of wrecked cars. Both are tempting and dangerous, but most of all the mother's world, where even the lacy flower "was nasty, the tiny black dot at the center, you'd think it was an insect or something."

Growing up female, smart, and wary in an environment where the female and the intelligent are natural victims, Marya struggles to destroy everything in her that bears the mother's mark, the mark of the body, of sexuality, of vulnerability. Sexually abused by her loutish cousin, mocked and harassed by the village toughs, she learns to close off her body, to become "not-there," and to deny her own desires for intimacy and touch. In high school, she thinks of becoming a nun. Yet the short stories she hesitantly begins to write frighten her. She dreads looking into the mirror and seeing "something forbidden: her mother's face, that slack-lidded wink, the glassy stare, the smile rimmed with lipstick and saliva," the heavy hair "like her own mother's hair."

The night before Marya leaves home for the university where she alone has won a scholarship, her waist-length hair—the mother's mark—is cut off by her drunken and envious classmates in a scene that is both a kind of rape and a rite of passage. In adulthood, as she becomes a successful professor and writer—the novel takes her to the age of thirty-six—she is a woman who is trying to be genderless, to deny the body and live in and through the mind. But every intellectual advance intensifies Marya's sense of estrangement. Unable to acknowledge the intensity of her longing for female affection, Marya helplessly repeats the patterns of her childhood, in affairs with older married men, who die and leave her abandoned but somehow connected to their wives, the lost "mothers" with whom she has unconsciously bonded.

Oates never idealizes the process by which Marya comes to the decision that at mid-life she must reclaim a matrilineal past. The community of women is not idyllic, but torn by rage, competition, primal jealousies, ambiguous desire, and emotional violence, just like the world in which women seem subordinate to and victimized by men. And we do not know what kind of renewal Marya's reunion with her mother will bring. The novel ends with Marya holding up the letter and the snapshot of the mother whose reappearance will "cut [her] life in two." This intensely moving conclusion may remind some readers of the famous freeze-frame at the end of Truffaut's "400 Blows," in which the autobiographical young hero on the run comes to the sea and stops, with nowhere else to go; except that for Oates's heroine the final frame is a powerful moment of opening rather than confinement. The mother's country may be a wilderness rather than a peaceful or paradisal garden; yet to refuse or to deny it is to be in permanent exile.

Chronology

1938   Joyce Carol Oates is born June 16 in Millerport, New York, to Caroline and Frederic Oates. The eldest of three daughters, she grows up on her maternal grandparents' farm in Erie County.

1956   Matriculates at Syracuse University on a scholarship.

1959   Co-winner, first prize, *Mademoiselle* College Fiction Contest for a story entitled "In the Old World."

1960   Graduates as class valedictorian, with a B.A. in English (and a minor in philosophy).

1961   Weds Raymond J. Smith, Jr., January 23. Receives M.A. in English from University of Wisconsin, Madison, and enrolls in doctoral program at Rice University. One of her stories is chosen for the Honor Roll in Martha Foley's *The Best American Short Stories,* which encourages her to favor her writing career over her graduate training.

1962   Appointed Instructor in English at the University of Detroit.

1963   *By the North Gate,* a collection of short stories, is published.

1964   *With Shuddering Fall,* her first novel, is published.

1965   Her play "The Sweet Enemy" premiers at the Actor's Playhouse, New York City.

1966   *Upon the Sweeping Flood* is published.

1967   *A Garden of Earthly Delights* is published. Appointed Assistant Professor of English at the University of Windsor. Receives the O. Henry Prize Award, first prize for "In the Region of Ice"; and a Guggenheim Fellowship.

1968   *Expensive People* and *Women in Love and Other Poems* are published. Receives the Richard and Hinda Rosenthal Award of the National Institute of Arts and Letters for *A Garden of Earthly Delights*, and a National Endowment for the Humanities Grant.

1969   *Them* and *Anonymous Sins and Other Poems* are published. Awarded first prize, Emily Clark Balch Short Story Competition for "Convalescing"; and second prize, O. Henry Prize Awards, for "Accomplished Desires."

1970   *The Wheel of Love and Other Stories* and *Love and Its Derangements and Other Poems* are published. *Them* receives the National Book Award.

1971   *Wonderland* and *The Edge of Impossibility: Tragic Forms in Literature* are published. Oates spends the year in London.

1972   *Marriages and Infidelities* is published. Oates edits *Scenes from American Life: Contemporary Short Fiction*. Her play "Ontological Proof of My Existence" premiers at the Cubiculo Theatre, New York City.

1973   *Do with Me What You Will, Angel Fire, The Hostile Sun*, and *dreaming america* are published, along with a revised edition of *Wonderland*. The play, "Miracle Play," premiers at Playhouse II Theatre, New York. Oates's story "The Dead" receives first prize, O. Henry Prize Awards.

1974   *The Goddess and Other Women, The Hungry Ghosts: Seven Allusive Comedies, Where Are You Going, Where Have You Been?: Stories of Young America, Miracle Play*, and *New Heaven, New Earth: The Visionary Experience in Literature* are published. Oates and her husband launch *The Ontario Review: A North American Journal of the Arts*.

1975   *The Assassins: A Book of Hours, The Poisoned Kiss and Other Stories from the Portuguese, The Seduction and Other Stories*, and *The Fabulous Beasts* are published. Receives the Lotos Club Award of Merit.

1976   *Childwold, The Triumph of the Spider Monkey: The First Person Confession of the Maniac Bobby Gotteson as Told to Joyce Carol Oates* (a novella), and *Crossing the Border: Fifteen Tales* are published.

1977   *Night-Side: Eighteen Tales* is published.

1978   *Son of the Morning* (a novel), *All the Good People I've Left Behind* (stories), and *Women Whose Lives Are Food, Men Whose Lives Are Money* (poems) are published. Oates is appointed Writer-in-Residence at Princeton University, and elected to the American Academy of Arts and Letters.

1979   *Cybele* and *Unholy Loves* are published.

1980   *Bellefleur* and *A Sentimental Education: Stories* are published.

1981   *Angel of Light* and *Contraries: Essays* are published.

1982   *A Bloodsmoor Romance* and *Invisible Woman: New and Selected Poems, 1970–1982* are published, along with *Nightwalks: A Bedside Companion,* which is compiled and introduced by Oates.

1983   *First Person Singular: Writers on Their Craft,* edited by Oates, is published.

1984   *Mysteries of Winterthurn* and *Last Days: Stories* are published.

1985   *Solstice* is published.

1986   *Marya: A Life* and *Raven's Wings* (stories) are published.

1987   *Boxing* is published.

Contributors

HAROLD BLOOM, Sterling Professor of the Humanities at Yale University, is the author of *The Anxiety of Influence, Poetry and Repression,* and many other volumes of literary criticism. His forthcoming study, *Freud: Transference and Authority,* attempts a full-scale reading of all of Freud's major writings. A MacArthur Prize Fellow, he is general editor of five series of literary criticism published by Chelsea House.

WALTER SULLIVAN is Professor of English at Vanderbilt University and the author of *Death by Melancholy: Essays on Modern Southern Fiction.*

CALVIN BEDIENT is Professor of English at the University of California at Los Angeles and the author of *Architects of the Self* and *Eight Contemporary Poets.*

GORDON O. TAYLOR is Dean of the Arts and Sciences at Tulsa University.

G. F. WALLER is Professor of English at Carnegie-Mellon University, Pittsburgh, and the author of *Dreaming America: Obsession and Transcendence in the Fiction of Joyce Carol Oates, The Strong Necessity of Time,* and a study of Mary Sidney, Countess of Pembroke.

EILEEN T. BENDER teaches English at the University of Notre Dame and is the author of a forthcoming study of Joyce Carol Oates.

MARY ALLEN is Lecturer in English at George Mason University in Fairfax, Virginia. She is the author of *The Necessary Blankness: Women in Major American Fiction of the Sixties.*

ROSE MARIE BURWELL is Professor of English at Northern Illinois University, DeKalb.

147

JOHN GARDNER taught English literature at Southern Illinois University, Carbondale. His books include *Freddy's Book, October Light, The Sunlight Dialogues,* and *On Becoming a Novelist,* among many others.

THOMAS R. EDWARDS is Professor of English at Rutgers University, New Brunswick, New Jersey, and executive editor of *Raritan.*

FREDERICK R. KARL is Professor of English at New York University. His books include *The Contemporary English Novel, Joseph Conrad: The Three Lives,* and *The Adversary Literature.*

SAMUEL CHASE COALE teaches English at Wheaton College and is the author of *In Hawthorne's Shadow.*

ELAINE SHOWALTER is Professor of English at Princeton University and the author of *A Literature of Their Own: British Women Novelists from Brontë to Lessing.*

Bibliography

Adams, Robert M. "Joyce Carol Oates at Home." *The New York Times* (28 September 1969): 4–5, 48.

Allen, Bruce. "Intrusions of Consciousness." *Hudson Review* 28 (1975–76): 611–15.

Andersen, Sally. "The Poetry of Joyce Carol Oates." *Spirit* 39 (1972): 24–29.

Avant, John Alfred. "An Interview with Joyce Carol Oates." *Library Journal* (15 November 1972): 3711–12.

Batterberry, Michael and Ariane. "Focus on Joyce Carol Oates." *Harper's Bazaar* (September 1973): 159, 174, 176.

Bellamy, Joe David. "The Dark Lady of American Letters: An Interview with Joyce Carol Oates." *The Atlantic Monthly* 229, no. 2 (1972): 63–67.

Bender, Eileen T. "Between the Categories: Recent Short Fiction by Joyce Carol Oates." *Studies in Short Fiction* 17 (1980): 415–23.

Bergonzi, Bernard. "Truants." *The New York Review of Books* 11 (2 January 1979): 40–41.

Boesky, Dale. "Correspondence with Miss Joyce Carol Oates." *International Review of Psychoanalysis* 2 (1975): 481–86.

Bower, Warren. "Bliss in the First Person." *Saturday Review* (26 October 1968): 33–34.

Burwell, Rose Marie. "Joyce Carol Oates and an Old Master." *Critique: Studies in Modern Fiction* 15 (1973): 48–58.

———. "The Process of Individuation as Narrative Structure: Joyce Carol Oates's *Do with Me What You Will*." *Critique: Studies in Modern Fiction* 17 (1975): 93–106.

Clemons, Walter. "Joyce Carol Oates: Love and Violence." *Newsweek* (11 December 1972): 72–74, 77.

Creighton, Joanne V. *Joyce Carol Oates*. Boston: G. K. Hall (Twayne), 1979.

———. "Joyce Carol Oates's Craftsmanship in *The Wheel of Love*." *Studies in Short Fiction* 15 (1978): 375–84.

———. "Unliberated Women in Joyce Carol Oates's Fiction." *World Literature Written in English* 17, no. 1 (1978): 165–75.

Cushman, K. "A Reading of Joyce Carol Oates's 'Four Summers.' " *Studies in Short Fiction* 18 (1981): 137–46.

Dalton, Elizabeth. "Joyce Carol Oates: Violence in the Head." *Commentary* 49, no. 6 (1970): 75–77.

149

DeMott, Benjamin. "The Necessity in Art of a Reflective Intelligence." *Saturday Review* (22 November 1969): 71–73, 89.

Denne, Constance Ayer. "Joyce Carol Oates's Women." *The Nation* 219 (7 December 1974): 597–99.

Dike, Donald A. "The Aggressive Victim in the Fiction of Joyce Carol Oates." *Greyfriar* 15 (1974): 13–29.

Ditsky, John. "The Man on the Quaker Oates Box: Characteristics of Recent Experimental Fiction." *The Georgia Review* 26 (1972): 297–313.

Doyle, James. "Cather in the Raw." *The Critic* (February–March 1968): 75–76.

Duus, Loise. " 'The Population of Eden': Joyce Carol Oates's *By the North Gate*." *Critique: Studies in Modern Fiction* 7 (1964): 176–77.

Ellman, Mary. "*Nolo Contendere*." Review of *Do with Me What You Will. The New York Review of Books* (24 January 1974): 36–37.

Engel, Marian. "Women Also Have Dark Hearts." Review of *The Goddess and Other Women. New York Times Book Review* (24 November 1974): 7, 10.

Fossum, Robert H. "Only Control: The Novels of Joyce Carol Oates." *Studies in the Novel* 7 (1975): 285–97.

Friedman, Ellen G. *Joyce Carol Oates*. New York: Frederick Ungar, 1980.

Giles, James R. "From Jimmy Gatz to Jules Wendall: A Study of 'Nothing Substantial.' " *Dalhousie Review* 56 (1976–77): 718–24.

————. "The 'Marivaudian Being' Drowns His Children: Dehumanization in Donald Barthelme's 'Robert Kennedy Saved from Drowning' and Joyce Carol Oates's *Wonderland*." *Southern Humanities Review* 9 (1975): 63–75.

————. "Oates's 'The Poisoned Kiss.' " *Canadian Literature*, no. 80 (1979): 138–47.

————. "Suffering, Transcendence, and Artistic 'Form': Joyce Carol Oates's *them*." *Arizona Quarterly* 32 (1976): 213–26.

Gillis, C. M. " 'Where Are You Going, Where Have You Been?' Seduction, Space, and a Fictional Mode." *Studies in Short Fiction* 18 (1981): 65–70.

Gilman, Richard. Review of *The Wheel of Love. New York Times Book Review* (25 October 1970): 4, 62.

Godwin, Gail. "An Oates Scrapbook." *North American Review* 256 (1971–72): 67–70.

Goodman, Charlotte. "Women and Madness in the Fiction of Joyce Carol Oates." *Women and Literature* 5 (1977): 17–28.

Gordon, Jan B. Review of *Wonderland. Commonweal* 95 (1972): 449–50.

Grant, Louis T. "A Child of Paradise." *The Nation* 207 (4 November 1968): 475.

Grant, Mary Kathryn. *The Tragic Vision of Joyce Carol Oates*. Durham, N.C.: Duke University Press, 1978.

Harter, Carol. "America as 'Consumer Garden': The Nightmare Vision of Joyce Carol Oates." *Revue des Langues Vivantes,* Bicentennial Issue (1976): 171–87.

Higdon, D. L. "Suitable Conclusions: The Two Endings of Oates's *Wonderland*." *Studies in the Novel* 10 (1978): 447–53.

Janeway, Elizabeth. "Clara the Climber." *New York Times Book Review* (10 September 1967): 5, 63.

Kauffman, Stanley. "Violence amid Gentility," *New York Times Book Review* (10 November 1963): 4, 61.

Kazin, Alfred. "Oates." *Harper's* (August 1971): 78–82.

———. "Cassandras: Porter to Oates." In *Bright Book of Life: American Novelists and Storytellers from Hemingway to Mailer.* Boston: Little, Brown, 1973: 163–206.

Keller, Karl. "A Modern Version of Edward Taylor." *Early American Literature* 9 (1975): 321–24.

Key, James A. "Joyce Carol Oates's *Wonderland* and the Idea of Control." *Publications of the Arkansas Philological Association* 2 (1976): 15–21.

Knowles, John. "Nada at the Core." Review of *Expensive People. New York Times Book Review* (3 November 1968): 4.

———. "A Racing Car Is the Symbol of Violence." *New York Times Book Review* (25 October 1964): 5.

Kuehl, Linda. "An Interview with Joyce Carol Oates." *Commonweal* 91 (1969): 307–10.

L'Heureaux, John. "Mirage-Seekers." Review of *them. The Atlantic Monthly* 224, no. 4 (1969): 128–29.

Liston, William T. "Her Brother's Keeper." *Southern Humanities Review* 11 (1977): 195–203.

Long, Robert Emmet. "*A Garden of Earthly Delights.*" *Commonweal* 87 (1968): 630–31.

Madden, David. "The Violent World of Joyce Carol Oates." In *The Poetic Image in 6 Genres.* Carbondale: Southern Illinois University Press, 1969: 26–46.

McConkey, James. "Joyce Carol Oates, *With Shuddering Fall.*" *Epoch* 14 (1965): 185–88.

Pagones, Dorrie. "Price of Survival." *Saturday Review* 47 (28 November 1964): 39.

Park, Sue Simpson. "A Study in Counterpoint: Joyce Carol Oates's 'How I Contemplated the World from the Detroit House of Correction and Began My Life Over Again.'" *Modern Fiction Studies* 22 (1976): 213–24.

Petite, Joseph. "'Out of the Machine': Joyce Carol Oates and the Liberation of Woman." *Kansas Quarterly* 9 (1977): 75–79.

Pickering, Samuel F., Jr. "The Short Stories of Joyce Carol Oates." *The Georgia Review* 28 (1974): 218–26.

Pinsker, Sanford. "Isaac Bashevis Singer and Joyce Carol Oates: Some Versions of Gothic." *The Southern Review* 9 (1973): 895–908.

———. "Joyce Carol Oates's *Wonderland*: A Hungering for Personality." *Critique: Studies in Modern Fiction* 20, no. 2 (1978): 59–70.

———. "Suburban Molesters: Joyce Carol Oates's *Expensive People.*" *Midwest Quarterly* 19 (1977): 89–103.

Pochoda, Elizabeth. "Joyce Carol Oates Honoring the Complexities of the Real World." Review of *The Seduction and Other Stories* and *The Poisoned Kiss. New York Times Book Review* (31 August 1975): 6.

Price, Martin. "Reason and Its Alternatives: Some Recent Fiction." *Yale Review* 58 (1969): 468.

Ricks, Christopher. "The Unignorable Real." *The New York Review of Books* (12 February 1970): 22–24.

Sale, Roger. "What Went Wrong?" *The New York Review of Books* (21 October 1971): 3–4, 6.

Schultz, G., and R. J. Rockwood. "In Fairyland without a Map: Connie's Exploration Inward in Joyce Carol Oates's 'Where Are You Going, Where Have You Been?' " *Literature and Psychology* 30 (1980): 155–67.

Stevick, Philip. "Remembering, Knowing, and Telling in Joyce Carol Oates." In *The Process of Fiction*, edited by Barbara MacKenzie. New York: Harcourt Brace Jovanovich, 1974.

Sullivan, Walter. "Where Have All the Flowers Gone?: The Short Story in Search of Itself." *The Sewanee Review* 78 (1970): 531–42.

Taylor, Gordon O. "Joyce after Joyce: Oates's 'The Dead.' " *The Southern Review* 19 (1983): 596–605.

Uphaus, Suzanne Henning. "Boundaries: Both Physical and Metaphysical." *The Canadian Review of American Studies* 8, no. 2 (1977): 236–42.

Urbanski, M. M. O. "Existential Allegory: Joyce Carol Oates's 'Where Are You Going, Where Have You Been?' " *Studies in Short Fiction* 15 (1978): 200–203.

Walker, Carolyn. "Fear, Love, and Art in Oates's 'Plot.' " *Critique: Studies in Modern Fiction* 15 (1973): 59–70.

Waller, G. F. *Dreaming America: Obsession and Transcendence in the Fiction of Joyce Carol Oates*. Baton Rouge: Louisiana State University Press, 1978.

Weeks, Edward. Review of *Wonderland*. *The Atlantic Monthly* 228, no. 5 (1971): 148, 150.

Wegs, Joyce M. " 'Don't You Know Who I Am?': The Grotesque in Oates's 'Where Are You Going, Where Have You Been?' " *The Journal of Narrative Technique* 5 (1975): 66–72.

Winslow, J. D. "Stranger Within: Two Stories by Oates and Hawthorne." *Studies in Short Fiction* 17 (1980): 263–68.

Wolff, Geoffrey. Review of *Wonderland*. *New York Times Book Review* (24 October 1971): 5, 10.

Acknowledgments

"The Artificial Demon: Joyce Carol Oates and the Dimensions of the Real" by Walter Sullivan from *Hollins Critic* 9, no. 4 (December 1972), © 1972 by The Hollins Critic. Reprinted by permission.

"Sleeping Beauty and the Love Like Hatred" (originally entitled "Do With Me What You Will" by Calvin Bedient from the *New York Times Book Review* (14 October 1973), © 1973 by the New York Times Co., Inc. Reprinted by permission.

"Joyce Carol Oates, Artist in *Wonderland*" by Gordon O. Taylor from *The Southern Review* 10, no. 2 (April 1974), © 1974 by Louisiana State University. Reprinted by permission of the author and Louisiana State University Press.

"Joyce Carol Oates' *Wonderland*: An Introduction" by G. F. Waller from *The Dalhousie Review* 54, no. 3 (Autumn 1974), © 1974 by Dalhousie University Press. Reprinted by permission.

"Autonomy and Influence: Joyce Carol Oates' *Marriages and Infidelities*" by Eileen T. Bender from *Soundings: An Interdisciplinary Journal* 58, no. 3 (Fall 1975), © 1975 by the Society for Religion in Higher Education, and the University of Tennessee. Reprinted by permission.

"The Terrified Women of Joyce Carol Oates" by Mary Allen from *The Necessary Blankness* by Mary Allen, © 1976 by the Board of Trustees of the University of Illinois. Reprinted by permission of the author and the University of Illinois Press.

"*With Shuddering Fall* and the Process of Individuation" (originally entitled "Joyce Carol Oates' First Novel") by Rose Marie Burwell from *Canadian Literature,* no. 73 (Summer 1977), © 1977 by the University of British Columbia, Vancouver. Reprinted by permission.

"The Strange Real World" by John Gardner from the *New York Times Book Review* (20 July 1980), © 1980 by the New York Times Co., Inc. Reprinted by permission.

"The House of Atreus Now" by Thomas R. Edwards from the *New York Times Book Review* (16 August 1981), © 1981 by the New York Times Co., Inc. Reprinted by permission.

"Modes of Survival" (originally untitled) by Frederick R. Karl from *American Fictions 1940/1980* by Frederick R. Karl, © 1983 by Frederick R. Karl. Reprinted by permission of the author and Harper & Row Publishers.

"Joyce Carol Oates: Contending Spirits" by Samuel Chase Coale from *In Hawthorne's Shadow: American Romance from Melville to Mailer* by Samuel Chase Coale, © 1985 by The University Press of Kentucky. Reprinted by permission of the publisher.

"Joyce Carol Oates: A Portrait" (originally entitled "My Friend, Joyce Carol Oates: An Intimate Portrait") by Elaine Showalter from *Ms.* 14, no. 9 (March 1986), © 1986 by Elaine Showalter. Reprinted by permission of the author.

Index

155

Love: hate and, 19, 114; "light," 21;
"Normal," 70; romantic, 79;
sexual, 41–42
Lowry (*A Garden of Earthly Delights*),
62, 63

McCarthy, Mary, 108
Madness: of Bobbie Gotteson, 123–24;
of Karen, 93, 95
Mae ("What Death with Love Should
Have to Do"), 66–67
Malin, Bernie (*them*), 111, 113
Mandeville, Bernard, 106
Manichean Bellefleur curse, 135
Manichean ethics, 133
Manichean vision, 123, 125
Manicheism: in American experience,
120; in *The Assassins,* 128; in
Oates's fiction, 119, 121; in *Son
of the Morning,* 131, 132
Mann, Thomas, 17
Marriage: American ideal of, 42; fear
of modern, 70; in "Puzzle,"
71–72; suburbia and, 41; value of,
55
"Marriages," Oates's literary, 58–59
Marriages and Infidelities, 36, 49, 56,
140
Martens, Nick (*Angel of LIght*), 106–7
Marya: A Life, 137, 138
Masochism, in women, 64, 65, 66
Materialism: of human personality, 42;
and mysticism, 134; and spiritual-
ity, 39
Max (*With Shuddering Fall*), 87, 89
Melodrama, 5
Melva (*The Triumph of the Spider
Monkey*), 125
Melville, Herman, 126
Men: in *A Garden of Earthly Delights,*
61, 62, 63; domination of women
by, 111–2; and fatness, 64, 65;
women's fear of, 67, 68, 69,
70–71
Men, and women, 15, 61, 62, 63

Mental illness: of Maureen Wendall,
15; of Clara Walpole, 13, 15
Metamorphosis, in *Wonderland,* 24,
26–27, 28
"Metamorphosis, The," (Kafka),
52–54
Metaphor, 27
Mink Pond, 133
"Minneapolis Poem, The" (Wright), 3
Minxs, Danny (*The Triumph of the
Spider Monkey*), 125
Miriam (*With Shuddering Fall*), 92–93
Miscarriage, in Jesse's worlds, 38
Money: 67, 93; in Jesse's worlds, 38;
Loretta and, 113; marriage for,
62; prostitution and, 78–79
Monk, "Trick" (*Wonderland*), 28
Moral maturation: of Karen Herz, 83,
84, 86, 87, 91; of Shar Rule, 91,
93; of Max, 90
Morals, 21, 50, 84, 96
Mothers, 8, 9, 10; as manipulators, 72,
73
Motifs, in *Bellefleur,* 101
Murder: in *The Assassins,* 100; of
child by mother, 72; of mother by
son, 73; in "Normal Love," 71; of
Old Rule, 84; in *them,* 78, 111; in
*The Triumph of the Spider Mon-
key,* 125, 127
Mutuality, Joyce's, 54, 59
Mysticism, 21
Myth, 19; of autonomous man, 54, 55,
58; of autonomy, 45, 47, 56; of
House of Atreus, 105–6; of iso-
lated artist, 47, 48; of personal
autonomy, 46, 47, 49; of self, 120
Myth-maker, Oates as, 19
Myths and legends, 135

Nada (*Expensive People*), 82. *See also*
Romanow, Nancy; Natashya
Narrative technique: conventions of,
141; in *Expensive People,* 10; in
A Garden of Earthly Delights, 12;

Joyce Carol Oates